D1733156

ART CENTER COLLEGE OF DESIGN

3 3220 00137 1603

The Complete Gnomes

Art Center College of Design
Library
1700 Lida Street
Pasadena, Calif. 91103

text by
Wil Huygen

illustrated by
Rien Poortvliet

The Complete Gnomes

Art Center College of Design
Library
1700 Lida Street
Pasadena, Calif. 91103

text by
Wil Huygen

illustrated by
Rien Poortvliet

The Complete Gnomes

398.21
H987c
1994

Art Center College of Design
Library
1700 Lida Street
Pasadena, Calif. 91103

HARRY N. ABRAMS, INC., PUBLISHERS

Introduction

Now, after twenty years of observation, we feel that the time has come to put our experiences and findings on paper, having received permission, of course, from an authorized council of gnomes—which, by the way, took all of five years to make its decision. It is our belief that this book fills a deplorable gap, for the published literature on gnomes is virtually nonexistent. One of the chief sources of information has been Wilhelm J. Wunderlich's bulky treatise *De Hominibus Parvissimis (Concerning the Wee People)* published in 1580. It contains a number of striking details, but, alas, confuses gnomes with dwarfs and dubious fairy tale characters so often that its overall reliability is negligible.

Today, gnomes are nearly forgotten beings. Since they work by night in the woods and sometimes in human dwellings, it is not sheer coincidence that the word gnome itself is derived from *Kuba-Walda,* which means "home administrator" or "home spirit" in the ancient Germanic language. In rural areas these home administrators often live in the rafters of barns, where, if they are treated well, they keep an eye on the livestock as well as crops. Another variant of their name translates as "to put in order" or "to do odd jobs"—with or without an apron.

In earlier times the gnome was an accepted member of society in Europe, Russia, and Siberia. Gnomes were seen regularly and people in all stations of life were rewarded or punished, helped or hindered by them (depending on their own attitudes)—a situation they came to find quite normal. But that was a time when waters were clear and forests virginal, when roads led peacefully from one settlement to another, when the heavens were filled only with birds and stars.

Since that time, gnomes have been forced to retreat into hidden corners above and below the ground, where they keep well out of sight, so much so in fact that belief in their existence is waning rapidly. Nevertheless, just as if you do not look carefully you will fail to see a hare in a meadow or a deer in a forest, so it is with gnomes: you may not see them, but they are there, all right!

Now that we are so concerned with saving what is left of nature's treasures, there is some hope that gnomes will begin to move about more freely. More and more people are beginning to realize that they have a neglected

but forgiving and wise mother in Nature. These people will undoubtedly meet gnomes. We dedicate this book to them in the hope that they will gain much pleasure from their encounters.

The gnomes consulted for this book were extremely reserved when pressed for answers to some of our questions, and as a result there are certain deficiencies or imperfections in our work. Valuable supplementary data from well-informed readers will therefore be most welcome. It will be included (with sources mentioned) in subsequent editions.

Although the woodland gnome is treated in greatest detail in this volume, other types are also dealt with. Gnomes, of course, are twilight and night creatures, and because of this we had to conduct our investigations in near or total darkness. Had we been completely true to our observations, many illustrations in this book would have been painted in blue or dull gray. To overcome this difficulty and provide an accurate picture of gnome life, the illustrations are colored as if the subjects had been observed in broad daylight.

Rien poortvliet

Wil Huygen

Art Center College of Design
Library
1700 Lida Street
Pasadena, Calif. 91103

Round about A.D. 1200, the Swede Frederik Ugarph found a well-preserved wooden statue in a fisherman's house in Nidaros (now Trondheim) in Norway. The statue was 15 cm. (just under 6 in.) high, not including the pedestal. Engraved on the pedestal were the words:

NISSE
Riktig Størrelse

which means "Gnome, actual height."

The statue had been in the fisherman's family as long as anyone could remember, and Ugarph succeeded in buying it only after days of negotiation. It is now part of the Oliv family collection in Uppsala. X-ray tests have proved the statue to be more than 2,000 years old. It must have been carved from the roots of a tree that is no longer known; the wood is incredibly hard. The letters were carved many centuries later. The statue's discovery and dating illustrate what gnomes themselves have always said—that their origins are early Scandinavian.

It was only after the Great People's Migration beginning A.D. 395 that gnomes appear in the Low Lands—probably in 449, when the Roman outpost of Britannia fell to the Anglo-Saxons and Jutes. Some evidence of this comes from the statement of a pensioned Roman sergeant, Publius Octavus, who owned a villa and farm in the woods outside Lugdunum (now Leiden, in Holland). He had married a local woman and so did not return to Rome. It was pure luck that his property was spared destruction at the hands of the barbarians.

Publius Octavus wrote the following description in A.D. 470:

"Today I saw a miniature person with my own eyes. He wore a red-cap and blue shirt. He had a white beard and green pants. He said that he had lived in this land for twenty years. He spoke our language, mixed with strange

the statue in Uppsala

words. Since then I have spoken with the little man many times. He said he was a descendant of a race called Kuwalden, a word unknown to us, and that there were only a few of them in the world. He liked to drink milk. Time and again I saw him cure sick animals in the meadows.''

In the chaotic times up until 500, after Odoacer, king of the Germans, had disposed of the last ruler of the Western Roman Empire, the gnomes must have established themselves in Europe, Russia, and Siberia, although exact information is lacking. Actually, gnomes find writing history uninteresting, or at least pretend to, but it is rumored that they have certain secret records.

In his book of 1580, Wunderlich mentions that in his time gnomes had maintained a classless society for more than 1,000 years. Except for their own chosen king, there were no rich, poor, inferior, or superior gnomes. This is perhaps why they made use of the Great People's Migration to begin afresh. It all sounds plausible until he tells of a map (now lost) of a gnome king's palace and adjacent gold mines; apparently slave labor was used in the mines, and sometimes there were slave revolts.

Using our scant information as a guide, we must conclude that gnomes gradually sought more contact with the people they lived among, and that they were completely integrated into our society 50 to 100 years before the reign of Charlemagne (768–814).

The adult male gnome weighs
300 grams

The adult female gnome weighs →
250 - 275
grams

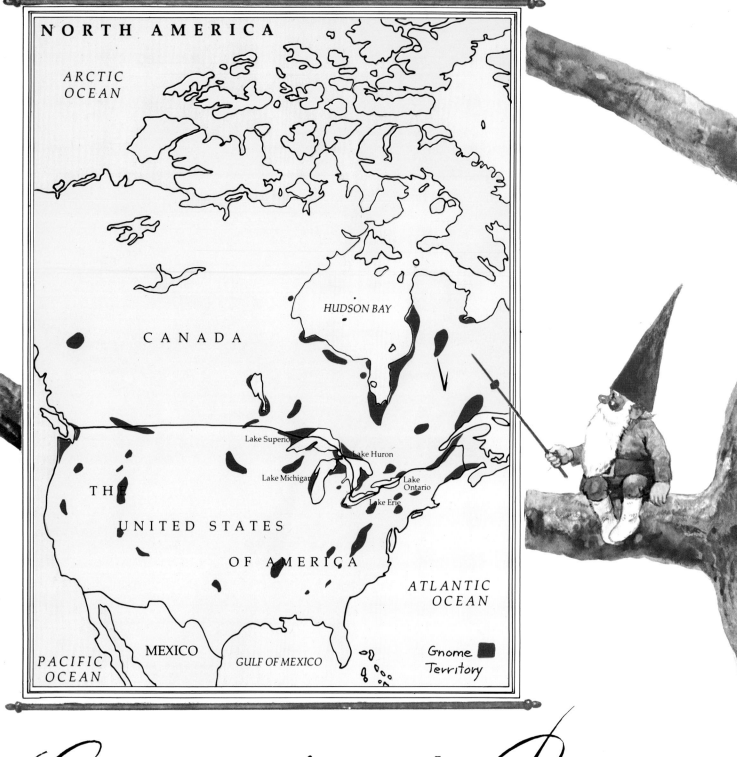

Geographical Range

Dispersion in North America

The map above shows a number of sites in North America where gnomes are reported to exist. The difficulty with establishing to a certainty that gnomes do indeed live on the continent has been that no sighting or encounter can be confirmed unless witnessed by two observers—the same criteria are used by bird watchers. Thus, though considerable evidence has accumulated, none of it is reported in this book. It can be surmised, however, that American gnomes (whose geographical range corresponds to their fellows' climate and life zones in Europe) do adopt the same dress, life styles, and behavior patterns as their cousins across the sea.

Dispersion in Europe

Western Border: Irish Coast.
Eastern Border: Deep in Siberia.
Northern Border: Norway, Sweden, Finland, Russia, and Siberia.
Southern Border: In a line from the Belgian coast via Switzerland, the Balkans, Upper Black Sea, Caucasus, Siberia. (This has to do with the shorter days and longer winter nights occurring in the lands north of the line.)

Names for Gnomes in Various Languages

Irish	Gnome	Polish	Gnom
English	Gnome	Finnish	Tonttu
Flemish	Kleinmanneken	Russian	Domovoi Djèdoesjka
Dutch	Kabouter	Serbo-Croatian	Kippec; Patuljak
German	Heinzelmännchen	Bulgarian	Djudjè
Norwegian	Tomte or Nisse	Czechoslovakian	Skritek
Swedish	Tomtebisse or Nisse	Hungarian	Manó
Danish	Nisse		

WOODLAND GNOME

275 years old
_____

in the prime
of life

actual height
(without cap)

15 cm.

his frowning
is due
to posing
in
harsh
daylight...

Tool kit
attached
to belt

Feet slightly turned inward to
insure great speed (over grass, etc...)

Daily dress —
Camouflage colors

ELDERLY FEMALE GNOME 346 years

(when 350 years or older she begins to show a light beard)

Physical Appearance

There are male and female gnomes. In our daily lives, we come in contact only with the male, because the female almost always stays at home.

THE MALE wears a peaked red cap. He has a full beard which becomes gray long before his hair does.

He wears a blue smock *) with a Byronic collar or caftan neck (usually covered up by his beard).

Around his waist he wears a leather belt with tool kit attached, consisting of knife, hammer, drill, files, etc.

Next, the brown-green pants and footwear

felt boots

shoes of birch bark

or wooden clogs

depending on the area in which he lives.

*)
The droll riddling rhyme from the opera *Hänsel und Gretel*—

Ein Männlein steht im Walde ganz still und stumm;
Es hat von lauter Purper ein Mäntlein um.
Sagt, wer mag das Männlein sein, . . . das da steht auf einem
    Bein. . . .

(A little man stands in the woods, still and alone;
His smock is of bright purple and with purple thread is
    sewn.
Pray tell: who is this little man, . . . who stands upon
    just one leg. . . .)

—has nothing to do with gnomes; it concerns a toadstool, most likely the fly fungus. The confusion probably stems from the unproven folk belief that gnomes, in times of danger, can transform themselves into toadstools.

Facial coloring is fair but with red apple cheeks, especially in old age.
The nose is straight or slightly turned up. The eyes are generally gray; the few variations are due to cross-breeding with Trolls in primeval times.

The eyes are surrounded by many wrinkles mainly

laugh wrinkles

which doesn't alter the fact that they can all of a sudden look penetratingly serious. Gnomes do not so much see the material presence of those before them; rather, they probe the real self and view the landscape therein to such an extent that no secrets remain.

Greetings, farewells and goodnights

are expressed by rubbing noses.

It is said that this allows for a more penetrating glance into the eyes. Hardly likely. It is probably nothing more than just a friendly gesture and, anyway, gnomes have no secrets from one another. In fact, they have only to glance at someone in the distance and right away they know what is happening in that person's inner self.

The gnome's conspicuous dress serves to
protect him from birds of prey during
the twilight and night hours. They are his
friends but could mistake a fast-moving gnome for a large mouse
were it not for his red cap.

Which only goes to prove that birds _can_ see colors, a fact
biologists doubt, even today.

On the other hand, his bright
clothing could be a disadvantage
when the gnome meets the more
annoying creatures of his life, such
as martens, cats, snakes,
Polecats, ermine, and hornets!

A night-hunting
owl →

Still, the gnome doesn't
fret too much about these
bothersome creatures, as he
far surpasses them in intelligence.

The gnome moves at such tearing speed—when he wants
to—even on long journeys, that he could easily
outdistance most predatory creatures, with the exception,
perhaps, of the hornet. The hornet, however, stings only
during the daylight hours, and the gnome is usually
indoors then. When a gnome has a daytime mission to
carry out, he first rubs himself all over with the juice of the
nux vomica, or vomit nut, plant; a small quantity of this
noxious material causes a tendency to vomit in all who
inhale it (save the gnome himself) and thereby discourages
the sting-eager hornet.

FOOTPRINTS

The footprints left behind by a gnome are very
distinctive—if you can find them! In order not to leave a
trail as he walks along, a gnome makes clever use of
pebbles, hard pieces of moss, and pine needles; by
stepping on them rather than on the bare ground he leaves
no tracks. Sometimes he walks in a circle or back upon his
own trail, or proceeds through the trees. If he knows for
certain that he is being followed, he will almost always
disappear into an underground passage.

    When forced to tread on bare ground, the gnome
makes use of a bird's-foot pattern printed in relief on the
soles of his boots. With this cunning aid he disguises his
travels. But gnomes sometimes give themselves away by
betraying the following small vanity: if you come across a
birch leaf on the ground with a clear blob of slime in its
middle, you can be sure that a gnome has just passed by
and exercised his skill in target spitting. He can't resist
proving his aim—and thus leaves a trail.

The clothing mentioned is worn summer and winter
without an overcoat, for the male gnome adjusts
well to all kinds of weather. At the most
he may wear an extra **vest** or **long johns**
during extreme cold.

THE FEMALE

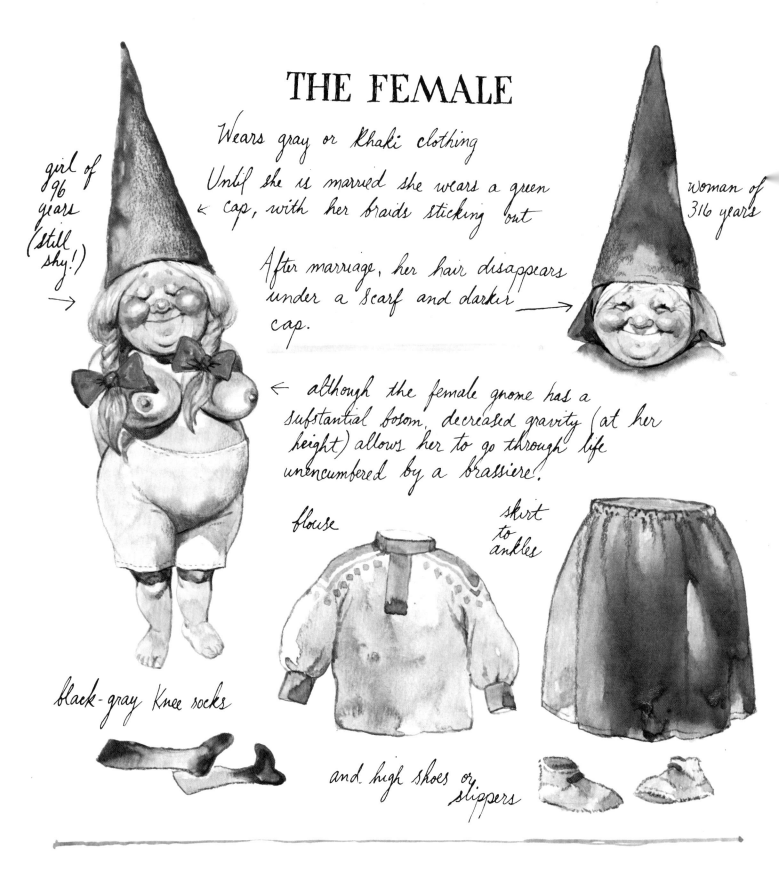

Wears gray or khaki clothing

Until she is married she wears a green cap, with her braids sticking out →

After marriage, her hair disappears under a scarf and darker cap. ⟶

girl of 96 years (still shy!) →

woman of 316 years

← although the female gnome has a substantial bosom, decreased gravity (at her height) allows her to go through life unencumbered by a brassiere!

blouse

skirt to ankles

black-gray knee socks

and high shoes or slippers

Mainly because of the gray color of her clothing, the female gnome feels safer indoors; mistaking females for small forest animals, owls could very easily cause deep wounds with their talons before realizing that they had attacked a friend. An advantage of the clothing is that humans have difficulty spotting female gnomes because their dress blends with the background so well. When a female gnome is picked up, she often disarms her captor by playing possum until she is released.

The Cap

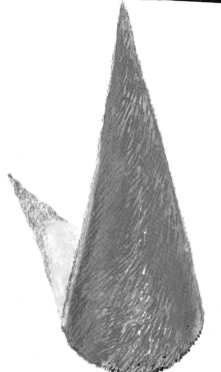

Deserves an extra explanation. It is made of felt and is solid from its tip to the top of the head (see cutaway drawing, left). The gnome never removes it except in darkness before going to bed and probably (although we have not seen this for ourselves) when taking a bath. A gnome without a cap is not a gnome, and he knows it.

Some folklorists insist that the cap has the power to render a gnome invisible, but if this is so, it is not its principal function. Rather, it is an indispensable head covering, protection against such unsuspected blows from above as are dealt by falling twigs, acorns, or hailstones, and against attacks by animals of prey. (Interestingly, just as a lizard will surrender its tail in order to escape, so the gnome will give up his cap to a marauding cat.)

The gnome reveals his individuality as much with his cap as with the shape of his nose. A gnome child receives a cap at a very tender age and keeps it throughout life. Because it is seldom removed, wear and tear on the cap is considerable, and with great care new layers of felt are periodically added to the outside. This work is done every few years with the help of a form molded in the exact shape of the gnome's head.

cross section ↓

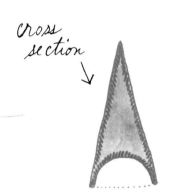

Gnome working at the **Cap form** a job that he hates!!

It is tedious work. But he would rather be without his pants than without his cap. (Notice that he covers his bare head with a cloth while uncapped.)

Physiology

Skeleton
Muscular system
Circulatory system
Brain and nerve center
Digestive system
Kidney and bladder system
Respiratory system
Connective tissue
Skin + hair
Blood
Senses
Hormonal system
Sexual organs

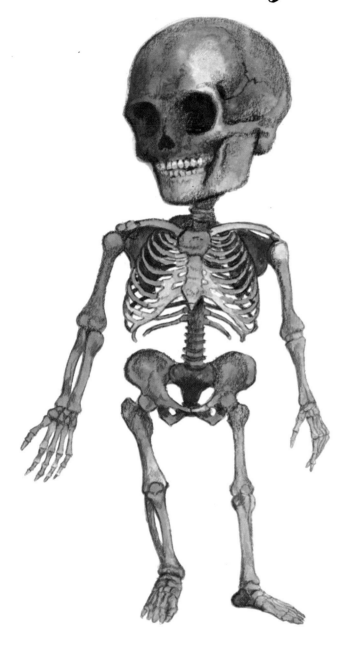

The brainpan is relatively larger than that of humans.
8 pairs of ribs, 4 floating ribs (humans, 7 and 5)
arms longer, legs shorter, foot bones and arch extra powerful.

Skeleton

Nature seems to find it necessary to produce two sizes in many of her creations: horse, pony; stag, hind; rat, mouse; hare, rabbit; and goose, duck. And so we have human and gnome; however, the difference in size is so extreme that the similarity is all the more striking. Following is a description of the (slight) differences in physical makeup between man and gnome:

Goose

Duck

Muscular System

Because—going from large to small—the volume, and therefore the weight, of an object decreases as the cube of its linear dimension and the surface area only as the square, even a fat gnome moves more easily than a man (compare a flea to an elephant). Gnomes can therefore run much faster, can jump higher, and are seven times stronger than man, relatively speaking.

Gnome leg muscles have an extra muscle bundle. Further, the gnome has two types of muscles—red and white. The white are for short-distance performance; they permit the accumulation of extra carbon dioxide, which is later discharged through panting breaths. The red muscles are responsible for endurance work.

Gnome with ears pricked up →

Muscular System

Because—going from large to small—the volume, and therefore the weight, of an object decreases as the cube of its linear dimension and the surface area only as the square, even a fat gnome moves more easily than a man (compare a flea to an elephant). Gnomes can therefore run much faster, can jump higher, and are seven times stronger than man, relatively speaking.

Gnome leg muscles have an extra muscle bundle. Further, the gnome has two types of muscles—red and white. The white are for short-distance performance; they permit the accumulation of extra carbon dioxide, which is later discharged through panting breaths. The red muscles are responsible for endurance work.

Gnome with ears pricked up →

7 times as strong as a man . . .

Circulatory System

Heart relatively large (athlete, race-horse).

Blood vessels, wide and of good quality (heart attacks are unknown).

More blood circulation than in man (adjustment to cold, power of endurance).

Hardening of the arteries known only after 400th year.

Brain and Nerve Center

Brain capacity larger than man's.

Digestive System

Total length of the intestines greater than man's (gnomes do not eat meat). Liver more robust, gall bladder smaller. Gallstones unknown.

Kidney and Bladder System

Urine can be contained for a whole day.

Respiratory System

Lungs relatively large and deep (power of endurance, high running speeds).

Connective Tissue, Skin, and Hair

Connective tissue extremely stiff and tough. Hair becomes gray very early. Baldness unknown.

Senses

EYE
Cornea,
lens,
iris,
retina (containing rods and cones).

Yellow spot contains 8 million cones; man has only a few and therefore has limited vision in the dark. The gnome, however, also has a high concentration of rods in the yellow spot, like the owl; this allows for sharp vision in the dark. Further, the very flexible pupil allows for maximum light intake.

EAR
External auditory canal short and wide.

Auricle relatively large and can be pointed in any direction and revolved.

Not tone-deaf.

Transmission to the brain occurs with greater electrical capacity.

SMELL
Mucous membrane to be found in *all* nose cavities, which explains the great nose size. Radio-light

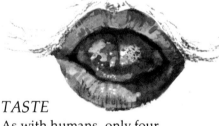

connection by transmission of smell to brain (dog and fox).

TASTE
As with humans, only four qualities are perceptible: sweet, sour, salt, bitter (the rest is "tasted" by the mucous membrane in nose).

TOUCH
Fingertips as sensitive as those of a blind person. Fingerprints are mainly of a circular pattern.

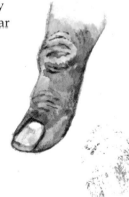

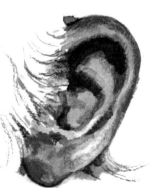

The World of Smell

Like animals, the gnome "sees" a great deal of the world through his nose. Even if he should become blind and deaf he would still be able to recognize his whereabouts and know what was happening about him in the forest: a familiar smell guides his every step.

Man no longer has this gift, though echoes of it still return in a spring breeze, the perfume of flowers, the scent of old farm villages, or a sudden smell of the sea, which somehow remind us of a happy youth, or of days gone by. City people use their noses only to take note of cruder smells such as smoke, perfume, food, kitchen smells, body odors.

The nose, however, is also good for "tasting" flavors. Except for sweet, sour, salt, and bitter—which are tasted by the tongue papillae—other oral flavors are transported, via the mucous membrane of the nose, through the throat and nose cavities for further discrimination (see PHYSIOLOGY: *Taste*).

For most animals (including fish and insects) the nose is just as important as the eyes and ears—if not more so. Gnomes' fine noses are used to seek out food (hyena up to 10 km.) and judge its value (the dog has an extra "nose" behind his teeth); for sex (butterflies up to 11 km.); for recognizing friend or enemy; for refinding their own tracks; and for orientation in unknown territory. In short, the nose provides most creatures with continuous information—information humans are obliged to do without. Our mucous membrane is no longer sufficiently powerful: it lies high in our nose cavity and covers only 5 cm.^{2}—a German Shepherd 150 cm.^{2}; a gnome 60 cm.^{2}. Or expressed in numbers of sensory smell cells:

Human: 5 million
Dachshund: 125 million
Fox Terrier: 147 million
German Shepherd: 220 million
Gnome: 95 million

The gnome, therefore, can smell 19 times better than man. Measurement with the olfactometer, however, reveals that his nose is actually 100,000 times better because of the finer quality of the sensory cells—as in the fox, deer, or dog.

Smelling something occurs when the nose inhales a number of molecules given off by a particular substance. For example, footprints have an odor caused by butyric acid. Butyric acid is a strong-smelling stuff emitted via the sole of the foot (also in armpit and on the skin). It can easily pass through a leather shoe; even after 48 hours a rubber boot is still saturated with the odor. With every step one takes, some millions of butyric acid molecules pass through the shoe sole, enough to be immediately identified by animal and gnome. Furthermore, they know if the scent is coming from left to right or vice versa. If they follow the wrong direction, within seconds they become aware that the butyric acid molecules have decreased (by evaporation) and turn back.

A good nose can register an unlimited number of smells; in fact, it can pick up the scent of anything on earth. To mention a few pertaining to the gnome: he can smell the types of trees, herbs, grasses, bushes, mosses; all creeping, flying, warm- and cold-blooded animals; stones, water, metal; and above all, of course, all activities pertaining to humans.

You are a keen observer if you can spot the doe in this landscape. But there seem to be no other signs of animals. At least to us. But for someone with a good nose there are all sorts of things to be discovered! (See next page.)

Let us "look" at this scene through the nose of a gnome on his way home at daybreak. Just as we can see this pebbly path through the woods on a fresh snowy morning, he can perceive (even in pitch dark) what has passed over and around it. Here are his observations:

Between midnight and 1:30 A.M., a badger trotted through (green dotted line).

Around 3:00, a mother fox took the path, leaving it here and there to sniff around (red dotted line).

About 4:00, a second fox appeared—a young male out courting (curving red dotted line).

At 4:30 a wild boar returned from grazing (blue dotted line).

Rabbits were hopping around all night (black dotted lines).

At about 8:15 P.M. the previous evening, two stags set out to graze (yellow dotted line)—and are probably still in the woods.

Fifteen minutes ago a doe began her morning ramble (pink dotted line).

These are the main things the gnome immediately observes. Many other details, such as the passage of two moles, the traversing of a weasel, the simple hopping of a hare, the rooting of beetles in the earth, the stepping about of pheasants, and the general activities of other small fry would certainly have caught his attention.

[As you can imagine, a cold in the nose is not funny to a gnome.]

EXTRASENSORY PERCEPTION

Nonverbal communication over great distances (fire, earthquake, flood).

Weather forecasting (thunder, storm, rain, high- and low-pressure areas); see THE GNOME AND THE WEATHER.

Sense of direction (as good as a homing pigeon, migratory bird). Compasses are not used. If a gnome receives one as a gift he generally hangs it on the living-room wall.

With the divining rod

Hormones and Sex Organs

Research in this area was difficult. In the literature everyone remains scrupulously silent on the subject. As well as ordinary adrenaline in the blood, gnomes have a type of super-adrenaline that makes for high-level performance in matters involving strength, stamina, and sexual drive. The sex organs are similar in form to those of the human. The female ovulates only once in her life. Exactly how that works, we do not know—but it probably became the norm through some magical intervention about 1,500 years ago. The male remains potent until about 350 years of age.

Illness and Remedies

Because gnomes live so long, one might presume that their blood pressure gets very high.

The gnome protects himself against this not only by using very little salt in his diet, but also by regularly drinking Shepherd's Purse tea. 2 grams of fresh Shepherd's Purse tea to 50 cm³ boiling water.

Shepherd's Purse

Because the males don't spare themselves and are active in all types of weather, they do have a tendency to

rheumatic complaints

Externally, they use <u>arnica</u>, and, internally, tea made from <u>dried stinging nettles</u>

Stinging Nettle

As a protection against flu and colds and infections of the bronchial passages, they brew tea from <u>Elder Blossoms</u>.

for gargling
Selfheal
Prunella vulgaris

Elder Blossoms

For curing diarrhoea and other problems of the digestive system: Poppy juice or opium extracted through a cut in a ripening poppyhead.

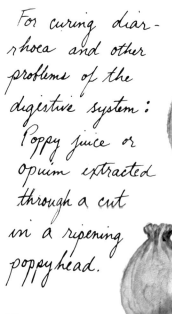

Poppy

Camomile or dill seed tea are used for curing insomnia.

Camomile

To prevent flatulence they drink fennel seed tea.

Fennel

A few pieces of dandelion leaf daily to help against constipation.

Dandelion

A daily leaf of centaury helps against hardening of the arteries.

Centaury Plant

To cure depression and general listlessness (doesn't happen very often) they use St. John's-Wort tea or the tea drawn from the white fibers of a walnut.

St. John's-Wort

To prevent kidney stones they use a tea drawn from a young birch tree leaf.

Birch Leaf

For the rest, they are not plagued with any other illnesses of importance.

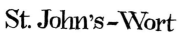

Injuries

For a
Broken leg
comfrey is rubbed onto the skin, and the leg is then set with sawn-off elder twigs.

Profusely **bleeding wounds** are staunched with yellow flag. Another good remedy is
Purple loosestrife

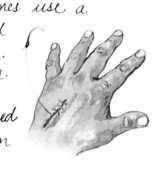

STITCHING THE WOUND
Just as we do, gnomes use a curved needle and boiled flax thread. Needles and tweezers are boiled in oil. Poppy milk is dripped into the wound as an anæsthetic.

FOR BURNS

1st degree : Rub on oil

2nd degree : (blisters) A brew of oak or maple bark is placed on the wound. (Gnomes have known for ages that freshly ironed and folded bandages can cause no infection.)

3rd degree : no statement (never happens)

FOR BOILS:
Tincture of **RANUNCULUS**
(Anemone protensis, L.)

Sprains, Strains, Muscle pulls:

An ointment made from arnica and leaves is applied.
Further, treat as for a broken leg.

Insect bites:

Vinegar made from fermented fruits.
Apply tincture of **Ledum**

(Ledum.-palustre)

Hornet stings:

Apply tourniquet, cut wound open, allow to bleed.

Snake bites:

Apply tourniquet, open wound, and suck out poison.

If this does not have the desired effect, or if one's life is still in peril, speedy transport to the gnome royal court is the next best thing! There, a Cure-all (a semi-sorcerer) has all kinds of antidotes at hand.

Transport of the Injured

If a male gnome is so badly wounded that he cannot move, he calls upon other gnomes for assistance by whistling a staccato tune taught him by his father. This special signal is used only in emergencies. Gnomes never "cry wolf"! The gnomes who hear the wounded gnome's signal rush to his aid, then transport him to his house on a stretcher made from two sticks.

If the patient's condition remains urgent, then the "transportation of emergency cases" phase is put into operation. One of the gnome orderlies rushes out in search of a hen pheasant, whistling in a special tone used only for this purpose. Meanwhile, two other gnomes weave a stretcher of fine birch twigs. Weaving time? Just 10 to 15 minutes! Two belts are attached to the head and foot of the stretcher; a third is connected to the middle (this will go around the hen pheasant's neck).

Then the fast fowl hurries at double time to one of the medicine men (half sorcerer, half doctor) at the nearest royal court. If necessary, she can fly over any body of water or danger zones in her path.

The gnome's life-span is around **400** years.

They lead healthy lives. They don't eat too much, have few emotional problems, and get plenty of excercise.

They do indulge in pipe-smoking and do not shun mildly alcoholic drinks!

Engaged couple at a party

The pipe, when being smoked, rests on the ground.

Drinking cup made from a stag's horn.

Growing Old

Even a gnome's life must come to an end. Over 400 years of age, the male rapidly becomes stiff and forgetful, though other gnomes still respect him. Eventually, the shriveled-up old man develops a tendency to wander. His wife displays the same symptoms, she being almost the same age herself. The housekeeping begins to suffer; the house starts to decay and becomes dirty and dark.

On one particular night, the aged couple does not return from their wandering. They have begun their journey to the Mountain of Death (never seen by human eyes)—and with the certainty of the migratory bird they will find it, if they are not attacked on the way by animals of prey.

As soon as they die, their birthday tree begins to get dead branches unless it is used by more than one gnome. (See TIMEKEEPING.)

Lives beyond 400 years or so have seldom been recorded, with the exception of a married couple in the Balkans who lived 550 years. But they were looked after for a great while by generations of a farming family, who placed a bowl of yogurt in the stable for them every day. They each had an olive tree on the Adriatic Sea.

Types of Gnomes

There are: woodland gnomes, dune gnomes, garden gnomes, house gnomes, farm gnomes, and Siberian gnomes.

Woodland Gnome

The woodland, or forest, gnome is probably the most common. But this is difficult to verify, as he is not fond of showing himself to man and has many escape routes. His physical appearance resembles that of the ordinary gnome.

Dune Gnome

The dune gnome is a fraction larger than the woodland gnome. He, too, avoids contact with man. His clothing is sometimes remarkably drab. The female of this gnome type does not wear gray clothes; hers are khaki-colored.

Art Center College of Design
Library
1700 Lida Street
Pasadena, Calif. 91103

Garden Gnome

The garden gnome belongs to the general type. He lives in old gardens, even those hemmed in between the new houses of modern "model" cities. His nature is on the somber side, and he rather enjoys telling melancholy tales. If he begins to feel too closed in, he simply goes to the woods. But, as he is quite learned, he sometimes feels out of place there.

Farm Gnome

The farm gnome resembles the house gnome but is of a more constant nature and is conservative in all matters.

House Gnome

The house gnome is a special sort. He resembles an ordinary gnome but he has the most knowledge of mankind. Owing to the fact that he often inhabits historic old houses, he has seen both rich and poor, and heard a great deal. He speaks and understands man's language; gnome kings are chosen from his family.

The gnomes mentioned above are good-natured, always ready for a lark or to tease; they are never malevolent, with a few exceptions, of course. If a gnome is really wicked—which happens only once in a thousand—it is due to bad genes that result from crossbreeding in faraway places.

Siberian Gnome

The Siberian gnome has been the most affected by crossbreeding. He is centimeters larger than the European type and associates freely with trolls. In certain regions there is not a single gnome to be trusted. The Siberian gnome takes revenge for even the slightest offense by killing cattle, causing bad harvests, droughts, abnormally cold weather, and so forth.

The less said about him, the better.

Every now and then a gnome family will inhabit a windmill.

GNOMES FROM OTHER LANDS

Karl May must have known the American
Indian gnomes,
but he didn't
mention them.

The Arctic gnome,
↓ chief of the settlement,
at -76°F.

Unfortunately the
clothes louse
(Pediculus vestimenti)
can stand this
temperature, and
the head louse
(Pediculus capitis)
is cosily
ensconced.

The Scots or loch gnome relies heavily upon whiskey to combat rheumatism.
He is friendly with the Loch Ness monster.

The Balinese or rice gnomes enliven the Emerald Belt with their dancing to a gamelan.

The venerable coolie gnome lives on two grains of rice daily!

It has been months since he had his last egg roll.

A Peruvian gnome in the icy, rarified air high in the mountains.

The blankets are made from llama or vicuña wool.

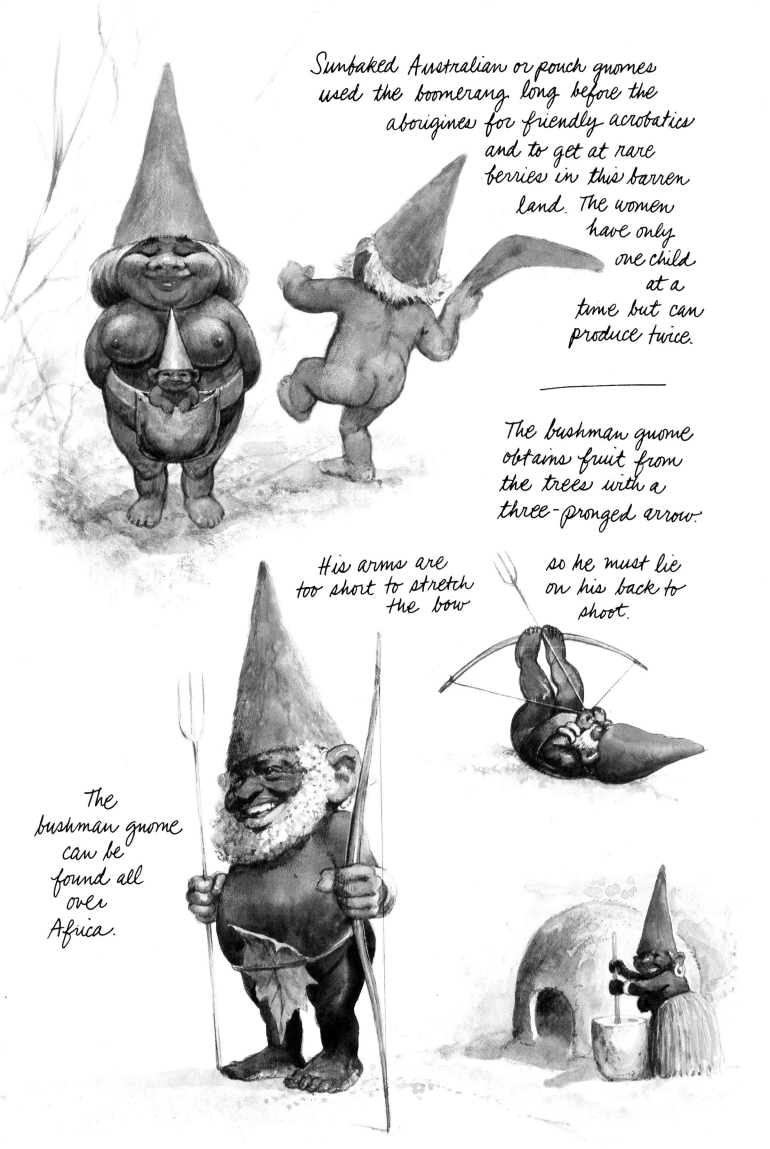

Sunbaked Australian or pouch gnomes used the boomerang long before the aborigines for friendly acrobatics and to get at rare berries in this barren land. The women have only one child at a time but can produce twice.

The bushman gnome obtains fruit from the trees with a three-pronged arrow.

His arms are too short to stretch the bow

so he must lie on his back to shoot.

The bushman gnome can be found all over Africa.

The Syrian gnomes
have kept the golden hamster
as a pet for thousands
of years.

This animal had
only been known in
western Europe
since 1931.

Hidden under the veil
is the exotic beauty
of the female.

The Papuan (New Guinea)
gnome is not the
friendliest sort. It could
be that not only his
nose bone
but also his costume
(that gets in his way
practically all the time)
contribute to his
ill humor.

An Orthodox Jewish gnome takes a turn with his Arabian brother after an endless wrangle over an orange consignment, although the wares have been tapped and felt and even cut open.

Greek → gnome, who after a good glass of ouzo and an ample portion of spanaki avgolimono (spinach with egg sauce), begins the Firtaki or Letkis (dances).

The Austrian gnome has to take off his plume when it snows or his cap would get top-heavy. A pair of knobby knees protrude from under his lederhosen.

It had not occurred to us on the flax fields at home —
there is lots of charm to be found in

Holland, our own
sweet little country:

the roguish
Volendammer

the reserved, shy
but pleasant
Staphorst woman
who can only
sing semibreves.

← two →
merry Zeeland
variations

a Bunschoten - Spakenburg

beauty
who can't help
smelling slightly
of fish from
the nearby
sea.

Timekeeping

Gnomes have their own secret way of telling time, based on cosmic oscillation. It is no trick at all for them to predict long-term periods of dry or wet weather, severe or mild winters. Excepting this, however, they use our method of timekeeping. Some of them have silver or gold watches. The cuckoo clock that hangs in every gnome's house is the traditional wedding present given to the groom on his wedding day.

A gnome keeps track of his age through the growth of an acorn planted in the ground on his day of birth. (A lime tree planted on the same day somewhere in the vicinity will do just as well.)

Cuckoo Clock

As soon as the tree is large enough, it is marked with runic writing by the parents. At the same time a copy is carved in a flat stone or on a clay tablet, and this plaque is given to the gnome in question on his 25th birthday; he keeps it in a secret place for the rest of his life. Very large old oak trees sometimes bear the runic writings of more than one gnome born in the same year.

Gnomes visit their birthday tree yearly on Midsummer Eve and add a mark to the runic script. Sometimes they even live under the tree, so they can easily check on their age when in doubt.

Gnomes snicker at man's superstition

"When the tree's big and wide
The planter has died"

They are extremely upset if their tree is cut down; but if that occurs they quickly plant a new one and continue to count on it.

Their adopted trees are never struck by lightning, storm, or disease. The tree begins to decay only when the gnome dies, unless, of course, it is shared by other gnomes who are still living.

Birthdays are not celebrated. The gnome sets aside an indefinite period of several weeks for quiet parties, during which he dwells on the fact that he is a year older. Upon request from faraway friends, he will extend these birthday weeks for an unlimited period.

Courtship, Marriage and the Family

When he is about 100, the male gnome begins to think of marriage; a small number do, however, remain single. The youthful gnome then begins to search for his girl. In doing so, he sometimes has to travel great distances because gnomes are few and far between and the number of eligible girls of his age not related to him is very limited. Plump womenfolk, round of form, are the favorite. If he does find one, he attempts to win her with all sorts of small attentions. After an agreement is reached with the in-laws to be, he will marry her. His house is given a rigorous inspection beforehand by his future father-in-law.

The Wedding

is a simple ceremony (except among the nobility)

At midnight, under the bride's birthday tree, the young couple, attended by parents and close friends, promise to be eternally true.*

*This always occurs under a full moon. If the moon disappears behind a cloud, causing darkness to fall on the festivities, they don luminous caps with a short train full of glowworms to ensure a few hours' light. These caps have been in the family for generations and are worn only on such occasions because this is tough work for the glowworms.

After the ceremony, the memorable occasion and date are engraved on an ornamental stone. Then the party retires to the young couple's house, where the stone is solemnly walled up. (The new house was furnished years before.)

After a festive dinner, the newlyweds leave for their honeymoon trip.

The honeymoon trip was discussed long in advance, with animals used for transportation and safety — wild geese, → swans, storks...

...foxes, otters, and in Siberia wolves — all do their share.

The honeymoon couple spend their nights in hollow tree trunks, rabbit holes, or uninhabited birds' nests. On their return trip, they visit the gnome palace and pay their respects to their king and queen, who like to know all their subjects by name.

Out of this union,
a pair of twins
is born, in the usual manner. Pregnancy lasts 12 months. Long ago – more than 1,000 years – families were much larger, sometimes 10 or 12 children. Due to a certain intervention, about which gnomes decline to speak, this is no longer the case.

The twins may be 2 boys, 2 girls, or a boy and a girl.

Since no deaths are caused by illness, the total gnome population remains about the same, with a slight tendency to decrease owing to the few who stay single and others who have fallen victim to accident or animals of prey. Gnome children wet the bed until they are 12; they live with their parents until they are 100 years old.

The gnome father leaves the upbringing of daughters to their mothers and limits his fatherly attentions to occasional horserides on his knee, → storytelling, Carving wooden animals

and playing games with them.

As soon as his son (or sons) turns 13, the gnome father takes him outside to teach him the many things every gnome should know:

KNOWLEDGE of mushrooms and herbs; how to distinguish between edible and poisonous plants, and friendly or dangerous animals.

How to increase his **Running speed** (to that of a hare.)

Methods of escape (in open terrain the so-called "heel slapping," or zig-zag method, and in wooded areas the use of mole tunnels, rabbit warrens, underground water courses, etc.)

Further, he is taught to handle the **Divining rod** which every gnome uses to trace water, locate treasures, and find earth rays.

Another important skill passed from father to son is **Whistling** shrilly — and loud enough to be heard at great distances — to warn of impending danger!

Gnome boys are also taught how to use a metal mirror to reflect the sun or moon's rays and flash messages when there is danger about.

Gnome boy of 81, already beginning to turn gray →

Indoors, the youthful gnome is taught all the tricks of the **Woodworking and Painting** *trades.*

At community forges and potteries (located in central areas in the woods and fields), the gnome student masters several trades—they feel that one can never learn enough.

When he is 75 years old, the son is introduced by his father to the members of the Regional Council, a few of whom he already knows. This initiation sometimes degenerates into a sort of hazing ritual that can cause him a few uncomfortable nights, but he eventually is rewarded with entry in the register and general good fellowship.

Girls are instructed by their mothers and neighbor women in the homely arts.

They learn cooking, spinning, knitting, and how to identify animals of prey—in short, everything a woman should know about running a home.

One of her favorite pastimes is cuddling and bottle-feeding the neighborhood baby rabbits, especially if their mothers have been killed by hunters or animals.

After the children leave home, the gnome father is again alone with just his wife—and this, after a brief period of readjustment, becomes quite agreeable. Family life need not be less harmonious because children leave home. If there is reason for celebration, gnomes from near and far will join in the festivities at the drop of a hat; the gossiping, drinking, eating, and dancing may last for days.

Gnome dancing is of the Yugoslavian sort: they move in circles, and there is much boot slapping and hand clapping. The gnome women deck themselves out with blossoms or berry-bearing twigs.

Special dress for dance parties:

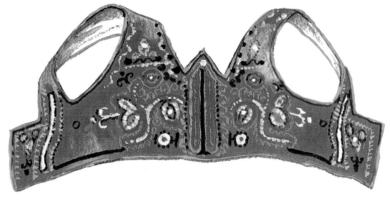

Attractive embroidered **Bolero** and "folk dancing" slippers.

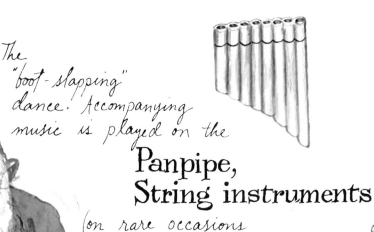

The "boot-slapping" dance. Accompanying music is played on the
Panpipe,
String instruments
(on rare occasions the violin), **flutes** carved from wood or hollowed rabbit bones, and a mouse-skin
Drum.
They sing along with the music very softly.

On warm spring evenings they love to let the thrush lead the singing, then they follow with their own **dreamy, melancholic variations** on that theme.

Later, when the thrush and blackbird are asleep, they thrill to the louder, more metallic, sounds of the nightingale.

Finnish gnome costumes for everyday wear and for Sundays.

Elimäki   Koillismaa   Sakkola Rautu   Kuorebesi

Kirkkonummi   Parikkala   Pukkila   Tuuteri

The scarf is also festive.

Muff and shawl come out of the closet when the weather calls for them.

During extreme cold spells a cape is worn.

Nor can the male gnome go without earmuffs. ↗

In the winter, long underwear is essential.

For the female less clothing is necessary in the summer. ↙

Simple but decorative, printed night things are the usual sleeping attire.

nightgown   nightshirt

(notice the mustache holder) ↗

Housebuilding

Gnome houses differ in style and location, depending on the area where they are built.

The woodland and garden gnomes live under large, old trees. The dune gnome makes use of renovated rabbit holes or else houses himself under pine-tree roots. If sand drifts expose parts of his house he covers them with pine-cone scales.

In earlier days, when the subsoil water in the dunes was higher, large pine trees produced grapefruit-size pine cones, and their scales made excellent roof tiles. Unfortunately, these trees exist now only in limited numbers.

Although the house gnome may have his residence in a garden, he can nestle down just as well between the walls of a house.

The farm gnome may live under the haystack—but here he must always be on the lookout for polecats. He sometimes resides in one of the supply sheds on a farm or under sloping planks or poles leaning against farmhouse walls—which through neglect sometimes remain in that position for twenty years. But owing to the danger of a polecat, cat, or rat, farm gnomes usually choose a well-built little house and make their home under the roof tiles, or somewhere in the stables.

Hidden Entrance

The Tree House

The gnome starts building his house 15 to 20 years before his marriage. First, he looks around for a spot in a garden or in the woods where lichen or beard moss grows. This indicates clean air, for otherwise these moss species would die (exhaust fumes, etc.). Using the divining rod, he makes certain there are no earth rays in the area.

Under the first stairway we find a polecat trap, a folding trapdoor. The gnomes (and their visitors) who come in and out are too light to set the trap in action, but the ferret, polecat, weasel, or rat, greedily entering the hole, immediately tumbles below through the trapdoor (after thorough punishment they are set free).

How the polecat trap works

S ⇐ N ⇒

well ↓

sewerage ↑

Next he looks for two oak trees not too far apart (if need be, he will use beech trees). Under the roots of one tree, on the south side, he makes a staircase, then digs a hidden entrance. From here he tunnels (with the help of a rabbit; see further on) a crooked horizontal passageway under the trunk; this descends steeply after a short distance. Then he tunnels horizontally to the second tree, and rises to where the rabbit has prepared a hollow for the house itself under the tree trunk (dug in such a fashion as not to damage the second tree in any way).

The main direction of the house will be north–south. Where the passage rises, he builds an ascending stairway, with a bannister. A gong and hammer are hung nearby. A welcome mat is placed at the bottom of the stairs.

A the gong
B front door
C boot room
D well with bucket
E cage with watch-cricket
F dowry chest
G insulation layer of doe's hair
H drying attic for fruit, etc.

I chimney and air vent
J carved portraits
K door to washroom
L sleeping alcove
M basket of pine needles
N toilet
O chest of dried leaves

P Christmas decoration (on table all year round)
Q mice pets
R hobby and guest area
S guest sleeping alcove
T trapdoor leading to secret exit

Boot room

The first area the gnome partitions off is the

He begins by planing the wallboards until they are completely straight and smooth; then he waterproofs the floor. Next, he insulates the ceiling and walls with doe hair, wool, and moss fiber, all bound together with tough blades of grass. The planks may now be nailed to the walls. The floor is made from trodden-down loam or planks. (Needless to say, he saws the planks from tree trunks himself. He has years of time for that.)

The Living room

After the boot room, we have the living room, with extensions for three bed alcoves (one for father and mother, another for two children, and a third for guests). A corner is reserved for the kitchen; spaces for a bathroom, a fireplace, a hobby area, and a very roomy toilet. This enormous living area is also planed smooth, and it is thickly insulated with wool, hair, and fiber; walls and floors are covered with planks and beams. Father's help is indispensable.

the **Chimney**

(also an air vent)
The chimney of the future
stove is connected to
a woodpecker's hole.

Moles are good friends of the gnome. Here, one digs a vertical hole, meters deep, under the future toilet. If, every time after use, dried leaves are thrown down the hole, the sewage need not be removed and in time may produce nourishment for the tree. In former times, the wall of the vertical tunnel was lined with woven twigs to prevent its collapsing. Today, round piping sections of baked clay are used.

Mole

In a corner of the boot room the mole digs a second vertical tunnel. This well will connect to a spring, pure subsoil water, or an underground stream. The gnome then builds a stone wall around the well opening. Gnomes make no cement but sometimes get it from men in exchange for something or other. A mixture of mud, ash, and cow dung is generally used to cement stones together. The walls of the tunnel are lined with earthenware pipe sections to prevent crumbling and pollution. The construction of underground tunnels is one of the most time-consuming occupations of the gnome builder.

When the house is finished –
after years of **patient, steady, skillful labor** –
it looks like this, starting below the second tree:

At the top of the second stairway we find a heavy,
attractively carved front door, which opens to the boot
room. The middle section of the door is composed of an
equally attractive iron grille against which an inside door is
attached. This inside door is mostly left open to allow a
light air current to pass through the house from the
hallway. This draft is produced either by the wind outside
the tunnel or by suction from the fireplace.

In another corner of the boot room we
find the well with a bucket on a pulley.
Along the wall are more buckets and a
tub; various pots and bottles stand on a
work table, above which hangs the cage
of the watch-cricket; he has sharp
ears and announces any creature
approaching from the outside passage.
The gnomes usually find the crickets
lodged in cracks between stones of old
chimneys. They care for them well and
give them abundant meals.

The bride's wedding present, a dowry chest, is placed in another corner of the boot room. The chest rests on low feet and is beautifully carved and painted. Departing visitors are given presents that have been stored in the chest. These may be natural things, useful implements, or writings to be pondered upon, such as an odd sentence, a poem, or a profound proverb that may take a long time to understand.

Dowry chest

A second door, opposite the front door, leads to the

Living room ➡

Upon entering, we see an oblong table on the right. At one side of it is a corner seat against the wall; on the other side are father's and mother's chairs (children *stand* at the table). A Christmas centerpiece remains on the table all the year round.

Farther to the right we have the play and hobby room, which also contains the guest alcove—big enough for two. The trapdoor built into the floor connects to an underground passage. In the play area or under the table is the basket for the field-mouse family that keeps the house free of insects and vermin.*

The gnome keeps 3 or 4; they are tame and house-trained like man's dog. The young ones are amusing playmates for the gnome children. When they are grown they are either exchanged for others or set free.

Because of the good care that they receive they are convivial companions. It is a pity that their life-span is so short.

*The Russet Field mouse is 9–13.5 cm. long. Tail length 4–6 cm. (80 rings). Its back is red-brown, stomach white. The feet are also white. The head is short and blunt; large eyes and ears. An excellent digger and climber. Every year the female gives birth to 2 to 8 young, who open their eyes after 10 days. Pregnancy lasts 17–18 days. Life-span: 2–3 years.

Russet Field Mouse

To catch small, annoying underground flies, a bog plant
(Pinguicula vulgaris) is hung from the ceiling; the flies are
caught on its sticky leaves.

Beyond the playroom is the door leading to the toilet room.
The door is beautiful—sometimes inlaid with precious
stones—but the comfortable "throne" inside is even more
beautiful. Neither labor nor cost is spared in its carving and
painting. The gnome takes his time when using this room
and meanwhile occupies himself with handcraft. Toilet
paper, made with the aid of the paper wasp, hangs next to
the "throne." Alongside stands a tall stone jar full of dried
leaves to throw down the hole afterward.

Toilet

The Large Stove

Back in the living room we find a neatly stacked woodpile for fuel. In a tall basket are fragrant pine needles used as an air refresher. (The gnome is very skilled in lighting fire; he uses dried tinder fungus, which grows on beech trees. With two flints he strikes the necessary sparks.)

Then we have the large, gaily painted chimney, facing north, and underneath it the stove, which is used for cooking and providing warmth. Spoons, pokers, pipes, and candle holders hang on the chimney walls.

In **PRIMITIVE** times,
they made fire by
quickly rotating sticks

← the oldest method

several centuries later
an improvement on
the same theme
(notice the caps
were gray then!)

Gnomes made oil paint from earth pigments* long before men (who invented and used it just before and during the time of the Van Eyck brothers—about 1400). Gnomes use paint for decorating furniture and the interiors of their houses; they do not use it to paint pictures. Instead, they carve portraits of their ancestors, loved ones, or celebrities.

*From earth and clay—cleansed, then mixed with oil. It holds up well in paintings and comes in ochers, umbers, burnt sienna, terra-cotta, Vandyke brown, etc.

As counterpart to the toilet room, there is an equally large bathroom. The wrought-iron tub is filled with buckets of water heated on the stove. Sometimes there is a shower connected to a reservoir of rainwater in the attic. The bathwater drain is connected by a sloping tunnel to the vertical sewer line. In the bathroom, mirrors of polished silver, made with patience and devotion—and just as effective as glass mirrors—hang on the walls.

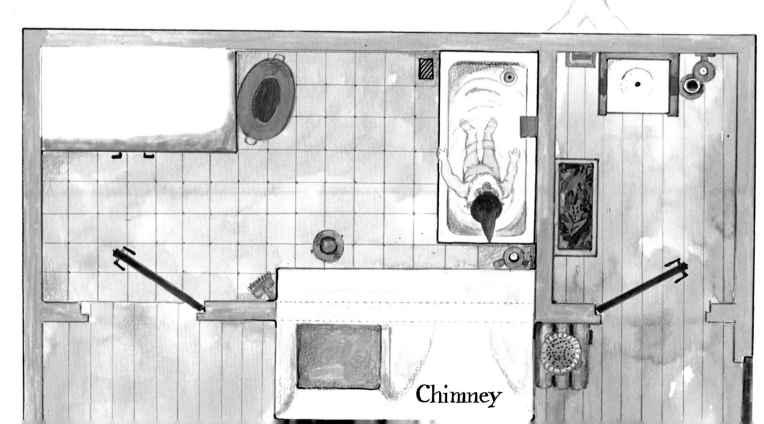

sewer

Chimney

Continuing in a clockwise direction, we come to the side wall where the family alcoves (cupboard beds) are situated, with a bench under each alcove for stepping up. Carved portraits and bed warmers hang on the alcove walls. Between the alcoves is a neat row of storage drawers.

Finally, returning to the living-room door, we find the cuckoo clock, found in every gnome residence. Every gnome bridegroom receives one when he gets married, as already noted.

The living room has a double ceiling. The space between is used for drying fruit; it can be reached via a small ladder and trapdoor. Hooks, for hanging a cradle in the living room, are attached to the lower beams.

The interior layout of every gnome house depends more or less on the position of the roots of the tree under which it is built. Some gnomes prefer a deep-lying house without windows, while others prefer a high window somewhere in a sloping roof—especially in soggy forests where deep building is difficult.

Wax candles are used to obtain light. The gnomes make them from beeswax (see HOME INDUSTRY).

Being on good terms with rabbit and mole has mutual benefits, apart from the joy of harmonious contact. These gray and black-velvet toilers patiently dig all the tunnels and passages needed by the gnome. A special advantage here is that they will never inadvertently dig up a gnome house because they know exactly where each one is situated.

In return for its efforts in tunneling, a gnome will always warn a mole if he discovers a mole trap in one of his passages, which the mole might otherwise not notice until it was too late. The gnome also advises rabbits to remain inside when there is hunting in the vicinity; furthermore, he keeps the rabbit company during his last miserable hours if the poor creature is stricken by myxomatosis. The rabbit's death cannot, of course, be prevented, but the gnome can mercifully give him pain-killing opium drops to ease his passing.

All gnome houses have, in one of the walls or in the floor, a special opening—covered with a cloth—connected to a rabbit hole. This opening also serves as an escape route in extreme emergencies.

Any part of the gnome house that protrudes from under the roots—for example, small storerooms in high subsoil water or drift-sand areas—is tiled with pine-cone scales, as mentioned earlier. Moss or lichen later grows over it, camouflaging it well.

The Third Tree

Under a third tree close to the house, the stock and supply rooms are built. Here the gnome stores his grain, beans, seeds, potatoes, and nuts. These supplies are indispensable, especially during long, severe winters. Incidentally, the gnome does not mind helping out any poor hungry wretch that has run out of food. The supply and stock rooms under the third tree are sometimes connected to the house, but not always.

A hilarious sight is a gnome busy filling his storeroom while behind his back a hamster is busy emptying it. Naturally, when this is detected, a lot of bickering follows.

Hamster

A snowplow
B earmuffs
C skis
D boot room
E hope chest
F tube cakes
G bathroom
H pump
I drainage pipe
J hearth
K air duct

L hand-held cleaver
M sauna
N sleeping alcoves
O firewood
P attic
Q rocking-chair cradle
R lemmings
S carved wooden "cock's tail"

Snowplow made to resemble the snow flea (Entomobia nivalis), an ancient insect one and a half millimeters long, that drills its way through snow in a similar fashion.

In weather below -4°F, gnomes wear earmuffs knitted from the hair of the woolly rhinoceros or the reindeer.

Their extremely keen sense of hearing is hampered by the earmuffs, and consequently they don't go as far away on their winter trips. In still colder regions, such as Siberia, they wear arctic caps made out of mammoth hair and with these the gnomes can face temperatures as low as -70°F. Their appearance is made very grim by these caps, and this is also an advantage.

Tube cakes (one half whole wheat and one half white flour) are made by pressing a hole into the dough with a mold.

The center part is used as a bun.

Gnome women have historically been better at this job than the men.

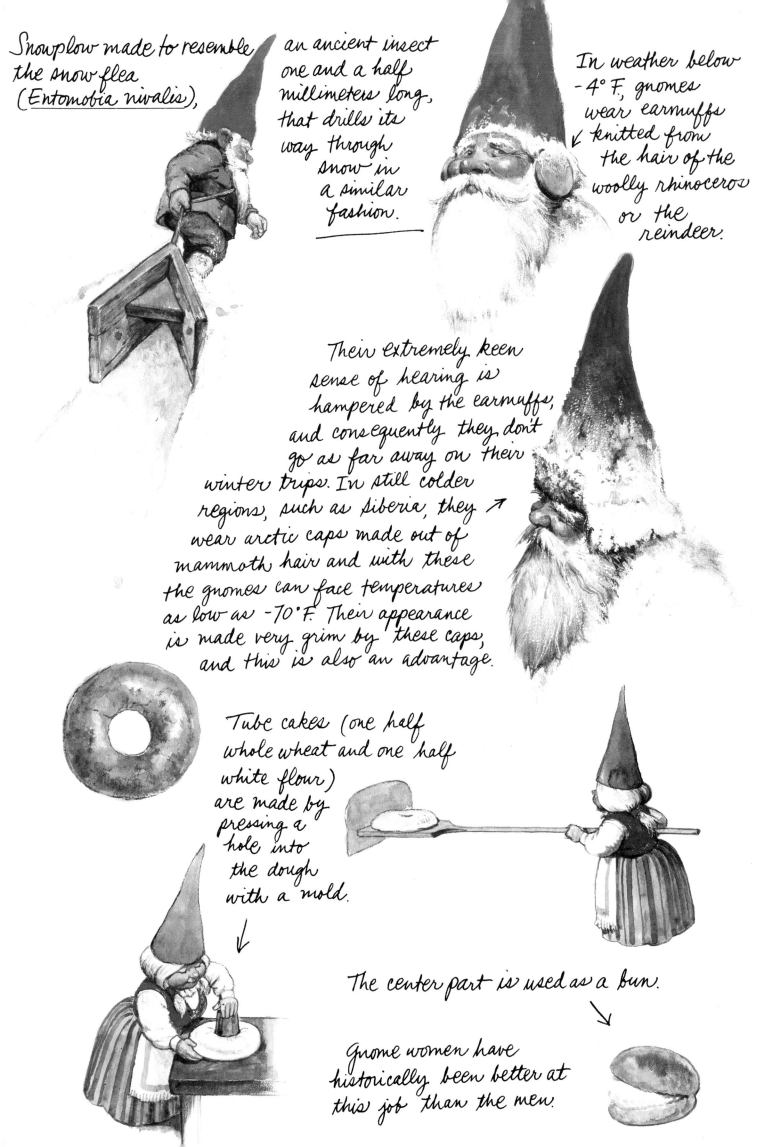

The hand-held wood cleaver nailed to the wall; the knife is so sharp that it slices through wood like butter.

The rocking-chair cradle is made exclusively for twins. One problem is getting up unnoticed once the babies have been rocked to sleep.

Without having to fuss with paper or kindling, gnomes can make a dependable little fire within two minutes by means of "rooster-cuts" in the wood. Larch wood produces the most beautiful curls. Christmas ornaments are made according to the same principle.

For a pet the gnomes keep the lemming, or reindeer mouse, an arctic rodent of the family of the field voles (Cricetidae).

When overpopulation occurs (every 8-10 years), these animals go on mass migrations, always from high to low-lying terrain, during which great numbers die as victims of predators and drowning. They do not hibernate.

Gnome dwellings in and around farms and old houses, although adapted to their surroundings, are usually of the same basic pattern. Again we find the polecat trap near the entrance. Rainwater is cleverly trapped in roof gutters and stored in a reservoir. The toilet and bath water is generally drained off into the manure gutters of the cowshed.

A variant of the basic gnome home is the willow house, which usually serves as a holiday house. Windswept (sometimes almost lying flat) pollard willows and poplars are used for this purpose. The gnome occupies about a third of such a hollow trunk. Ducks also nest in these trees and apparently feel greatly reassured by the gnomes' presence—especially while they are off their guard, bathing or eating.

Daily Routine

After sunset the gnome house comes to life (even without windows, they know when it begins to get dark — and besides, the field mice begin to toddle about then). The lady of the house steps out of the alcove bed, puts on her slippers, and shuffles off to the stove, where she gets the fire under way by adding dry leaves to the embers.

Next, she puts a couple of pails of water on to heat (if her husband wants a bath, that is) and a kettle on for tea. She then goes to the bathroom to make herself presentable.

When she leaves the bathroom,
her husband waits a few
minutes, then pokes his feet out
of the alcove bed (sometimes with
morning mumbles and grumbles).

He then steps into his slippers,
and hangs his nightshirt and nightcap on
a handsome wrought-iron peg. He looks on approvingly as his wife empties hot water into the tub;
testing the temperature, he then steps into his bath.

In bathing, he takes a couple of handfuls
of dried SOAPWORT (Saponaria
officinalis) from a tray hanging on the
wall and splashes it about in the
water to produce an abundance of
suds.

While mother and father are thus occupied, the children set the table.

In the meantime, father dries himself.

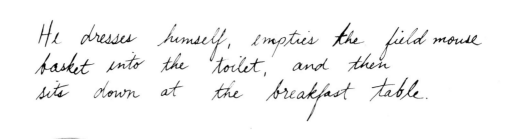

He dresses himself, empties the field mouse
basket into the toilet, and then
sits down at the breakfast table.

Breakfast is as follows :

A Mint tea
Rose-hip tea
Linden-blossom tea
Jasmine tea
} *any of these*

Rose hips

B Eggs *from small songbirds*

C Mushrooms *(various sorts as illustrated)*

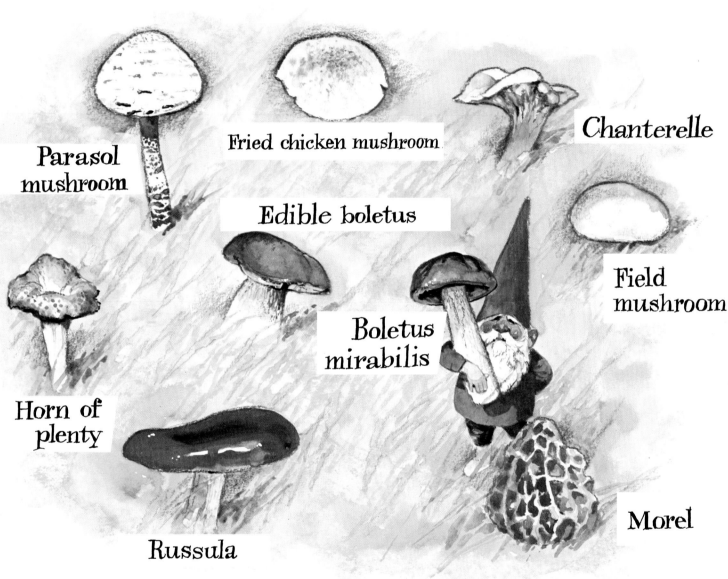

Parasol mushroom

Fried chicken mushroom

Chanterelle

Edible boletus

Field mushroom

Horn of plenty

Boletus mirabilis

Morel

Russula

D Butter *from sunflower or turnip oil*
E Porridge *made from various grass seeds*
F Bread *from acorn meal*
G Ant eggs
H Jam *foxberry, blueberry, raspberry, or blackberry*
I Spice cake

the sugar used is made from honey or sugar beets

His wife prepares a snack for his night journey— a hollowed acorn filled with tea and a bag of biscuits. The biscuits, baked from various grass seeds, are a hearty meal in themselves.

He lights his first pipe, waits until his wife has cleared away the breakfast things, and then they discuss the coming nightly activities or problems concerning the children.

On leaving the house, he pats the watch-cricket, walks through the long passage, climbs up the short stairway and "checks out" the terrain for a few minutes.

Check Out = *prolonged careful listening and watching*

If it is not yet
dark enough, the
gnome waits beside a friendly rabbit until deeper
darkness falls...

Anything may happen, depending on what he encounters or what his particular job for the evening may be. He could go to the forge, pottery, or

Sawmill

The roof tiles of these buildings are made from pine-cone scales.

Or, he may go to his herb garden and either sow seeds, weed, hoe, prune, or harvest.

He may take care of the firewood supply — or pick berries...

In short, everything that can be done during short, sultry summer nights, long, cold winter nights, velvet black or moonlit nights, rainy nights, etc.

If snow has fallen he straps on his long-distance skis. These are absolutely necessary, otherwise he would sink right into the snow, especially when it is fresh!

A gnome likes to keep his feet dry.

From a standing position he ↙ can easily jump thirty inches, just like a frog, and with a run, he can jump almost eight feet! ↗

Should the brush or the sogginess on a river bank prevent a run,
he will vault with a pole over incredible distances ↓ — and land on the other side —

dry as a cork.

The otter (see GNOMES) is a faithful ferryman. ↓

Floats are assembled without a nail.

Although the gnome hates to swim, it is sometimes necessary.

The belt is useful for keeping clothes and baggage dry.

Even in snow and ice
the gnome does not
sink (except in soupy
melting snow)
and is not
held up.

Downhill skiing
and
ski-jumping
are his favorite ways
of getting about.

If it is getting late, he whistles for a pheasant.

Then there is the cargo sleigh in all forms and the prick sleigh (sometimes you can see the pinpricks in the snow by looking carefully).

Ice dancing is very much in vogue.

Unencumbered by knots, ropes,
picks, etc., the gnome goes up
and down the steepest slopes.
He goes down quicker than up:
without tacking,
he makes use
of every unevenness
with his stick
and descends
in a straight
line.

Air travel

is for long journeys or for
flying over young plantations
to examine choked rivers, floods,
and to take note of decreases
or increases in green.
Usually the whole family
makes a day of it.

The stork provides trustworthy transport

though only in
spring and summer.
—
The misconception that
newborn babies are
delivered by the stork
is a result of faulty
observation.

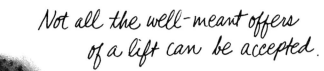

Not all the well-meant offers
of a lift can be accepted.

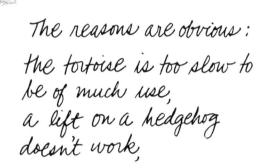

The reasons are obvious:
the tortoise is too slow to
be of much use,
a lift on a hedgehog
doesn't work,

and a
squirrel is
full of fleas.

It makes no difference to
the gnome whether
← it's light
or dark. →
He sees everything.

Even in dark passages under the ground (earthman)
he knows his way.

If he wants to cross a field unseen he just
tunnels through the snow with his sharply
pointed cap
(to practiced observers his trail is
quite clear).

If necessary the gnome can do this
in loose earth
↓

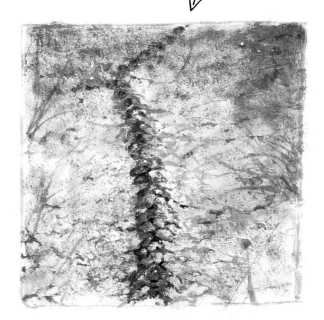

but too often these shallow
runs are considered mole
furrows, so you can't be
careful enough before setting
out a mole trap!

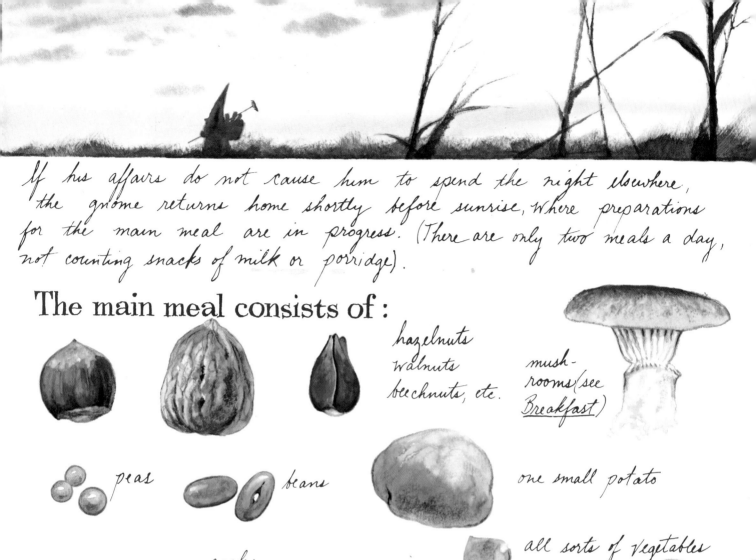

If his affairs do not cause him to spend the night elsewhere, the gnome returns home shortly before sunrise, where preparations for the main meal are in progress. (There are only two meals a day, not counting snacks of milk or porridge).

The main meal consists of:

hazelnuts
walnuts
beechnuts, etc.

mushrooms (see Breakfast)

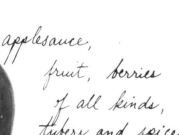

peas

beans

one small potato

all sorts of vegetables

applesauce,
fruit, berries
of all kinds,
tubers and spices

beverages

The gnome eats no meat, and so he regularly partakes of the high protein plant vetch (Vicia sepium), which also contains a nourishing nectar in its leaves.

mead dew
(fermented
honey)

fermented raspberries
(sometimes with too high an
alcoholic content, alas!)

nightcap:
spiced gin

dessert: preserves

Children are breast-fed for several years

His wife meanwhile spends the night (if she has babies) changing and washing diapers, ironing, rocking the cradle, breast-feeding and singing songs— or else playing games, cooking, knitting, weaving, dusting, making beds, chatting with the rabbits, passing the time of day with neighbor women, feeding the watch-cricket or grumbling at the field mice.

As the sun rises, the father gnome reads a chapter from the

SECRET BOOK

This is respectfully listened to by all. After that, the doors are bolted, the fire extinguished, children put to bed, and the field mice silenced.

And so the sun rises above the gnome dwelling. The bedded-down gnomes bid one another *slitzweitz* (their word for "goodnight"). There is muffled giggling in the children's alcove for a while, snores gradually rise from the parents' alcove, the field mice attempt to find a more comfortable sleeping position in their basket, the kettle cools on the fireplace, and in the boot room the watch-cricket contentedly chirps his one song. All is safe. Outside villains may lurk; storms, thunder, rain may erupt; animals of prey may abound. But above the sturdy gnome house a great tree stands erect; the alert watch-cricket, mole, and rabbit will immediately give warning if necessary. Nothing can possibly happen.

At every new moon the gnome awakes in the middle of the day. He steps cautiously out of bed and fetches the large Family Book. He sits down at the table and records any unusual events that may have occurred during the previous four weeks. He uses ink made from the inky cap mushroom. The book is delivered to the palace every so often for the king's perusal; it enables him to keep abreast of the activities of his subjects.

Home Industry

Lighting

Gnome houses and underground passages are lighted with **candles** and **oil lamps**

Gnome houses and underground passages are lighted by candles and oil lamps. The gnome makes the candles himself from beeswax: he keeps his beehives—small colonies—in hidden places in the woods and fields. To furnish a new hive, he rolls thin, cell-patterned sheets of wax and sets them upright in the hive. (He makes the cell patterns by pressing hexagonal pipes onto the wax sheets.) The bees build further on this pattern. The cell walls are made of wax, which the bees (fewer than 20,000) ''sweat'' out from wax glands in their abdomens.

The raw material for wax is pollen, eaten by the bees. Eggs are laid in the cells and sealed off by birth membrane. After many births, the incubation cells eventually become black, owing to the constant traffic of the bees, and must be removed. The gnome turns the hive upside down and cuts out the old cells. He places them in a metal box with a drainage pipe attached underneath. The lid is made of a double plate of glass. This apparatus is set in the sun. Under the drainage pipe he places a candle mold with a wick hung in the middle. The temperature in the metal box rises rapidly in the sun's heat and before long the melted wax begins to flow from the pipe, filling the candle mold. Upon cooling, the candle shrinks and is easily removed from the mold, its wick already in place.

wax sheet

In melting wax for his candles, the gnome must, of course, be outside during the day, and expose himself to harsh sunlight, to which he is unaccustomed. For protection he wears **Sun goggles** (similar to those used by Eskimos) made from a small strip of wood with a narrow slit.

Ceramics

The gnome makes all his own crockery. The material used is natural clay.* There are three forms of water present in clay:

1. Water chemically bound to silicate.
2. Water sucked up hygroscopically by the clay.
3. Water added to make the clay soft and pliable.

After an object (for example, a dish) has been shaped by hand, the water is eliminated in reverse order. First, the water added by the gnome is dried out in the sun and wind; next, heat up to 150° C is used to eliminate the hygroscopic water; finally, the actual firing, with heat up to 800° C eliminates the water in the silicate. The resulting product contains only silicate and is hard and durable. It has also shrunk 20 to 40 percent.

Owing to the natural impurities present (mainly from oxides), the end product is a red-brown color.

If the gnome adds calcium the color becomes lighter, almost yellow. This type of earthenware is called terra-cotta.

The more natural silicates present (calcium, potassium, carbon, or sulphur), the less porous the product. To avoid excessive shrinkage in the kiln (which results in cracking), ground sand or limestone is added to the clay while it is being kneaded.

*Clay is composed of hydrous aluminum silicate together with various natural impurities.

Under the eternal drip.

In ancient days, bowls and other utensils were made by placing a pebble under a constantly dripping water source; eventually the water's action eroded a hollow in the stone. Nowadays a potter's wheel is used with clay.

The wheel rotates via a pedal mechanism. Plates, pots, vases, cups, and bowls are fashioned this way.

Spouts and handles are attached later.

Before firing, decorative patterns are pressed into the wet clay with carved wooden stamps. Painting is done after baking.

Potter's Kiln

Baking pottery over an open fire or in a hole in the ground has long been replaced by the kiln. The firing process requires heat up to 800° C, and this can be obtained only in a closed oven.

Other household utensils, including cups and saucers, are manufactured by gnome craftsmen from hollowed-out deer antlers. Knife handles, forks, spoons, and buttons are also lovingly carved from antlers.

Glassblowing

Glass is obtained by melting rock crystals. All glass objects used by the gnome are of quartz glass—a much higher quality than ordinary glass. Quartz glass does not break in extreme heat or cold; it hardly ever cracks and has a natural sparkle. The blowing must occur under extremely high temperatures.

In order to color glass, the gnome liberally adds to the melted crystal the minerals amethyst, yellow topaz, agate, red heliotrope, and green plasma. He also makes marbles for the children from these stones.

The very clearest quartz glass is used for spectacles, telescopes, drinking glasses, and window panes. Variously colored or clear glass is used for indoor or outdoor lamps or lanterns. Interestingly, the lanterns are shaped in the form of a gnome's head (with a cap, of course).

Metalwork

Gold, silver, copper, and iron are used. Gold and silver have no monetary value for the gnome, but he gladly and frequently uses them because of their durability in all types of weather and their appealing luster. There are large supplies of precious metal in royal homes and elsewhere (the origin of which is not certain), and every gnome may take as much as he needs.

The same applies to copper. This metal is collected in its natural state in Sweden and Hungary and then transported to central depots.

Iron is obtained from melting hematite, an ore that contains Fe_2O_3 (red-brown ferric oxide). The furnace, a round stone cylinder about 30 cm. high, is filled with layers of charcoal and finely beaten iron ore. When the furnace is lit, the fire is powerfully fanned with a series of bellows. After some time, the iron melts out and the liquid metal can be poured off. After various purification and remelting processes, it can be fashioned into wrought or cast iron.

The method for casting utility objects of gold, silver, copper, or iron is the cire-perdue method, an ancient process still in use. First, a wax model of the object required is shaped, then it is covered with clay, in which a small hole is made. The clay is heated until it hardens. In the meantime the wax melts and drains away through the hole, leaving a cavity inside the clay mold that is exactly the shape of the desired object. (This is why the process is called cire-perdue, or "lost-wax.") Molten metal is then poured into the empty clay mold. After cooling, the clay form is broken and discarded, and the finished piece stands revealed, requiring only polishing.

Carpentry

The gnome is a born carpenter and joiner. He makes all his own furniture—cupboards, chairs, benches, and so on—without using a single nail. Everything is constructed with dovetail joints, wooden dowels, and glue. Little metal hardware is used; even cupboard doors are hinged by vertical wooden pins at top and bottom.

Constructing **bird houses** is a labor of love for the gnome.

All are made to measure. We see them hanging in isolated places in the woods. Out of gratitude, nesting birds allow the gnome to examine their eggs and take home any unfertilized specimens to eat.

When walking in the woods, please take note of any tiny holes you may see in tree trunks.

They are caused by the gnome's special **"pole-climbing"** shoes.

FLAX or LINSEED

Gnome housewives make all the family clothing. They weave flax into linen.

Clothmaking

Gnomes plant flaxseed in a secret garden, taking care to place seeds very close together to prevent the stalks' branching out. After a period of growth, all unripe yellow stalks are removed. These are then rippled to eliminate the seeds.

The stalks are now subjected to a rotting-fermentation process and then dried. Flax fibers are then separated through a metal comb, flattened, and rolled into balls.

The gnome wife spins the prepared flax into thread very finely, and after twining it, weaves it on her loom.

Doe hair is used to make wool (especially when it is strong and stiff). The gnome wife knits underwear, stockings, socks, gloves, and scarves. **Doe hair** is readily available, of course, to the woodland gnome.

For softer articles, the gnome is
permitted to take as much loose
hair from a rabbit's nest as he
requires...

Stray pieces of sheep wool found blowing in the fields or caught on
barbed-wire fences are used to make heavy blankets and sweaters.

Each of these types of wool is washed, oiled, dried, combed, hackled, spun, twisted, and knitted or woven.

WOOL DYEING

of the various sorts proceeds as follows:

for use **Hemp agrimony**

for **YELLOW** use **Sawwort** (*serratula tinctoria*) or **Columbine leaves**

for use **Indigo** (*Isatis tinctoria*) (the powder derived from this indigo plant is originally copper-red but turns blue through oxidation.)

The gnome wife can also make wool from **Thistle Down** which produces fuzzy balls from which fibers may be carded.

Basketry and Weaving

the so-called "round weave" for circular forms

circular woven floor mat

plaited basketry

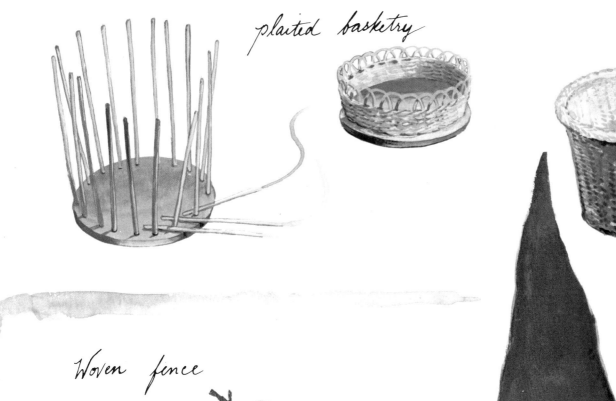

Woven fence (the technique speaks for itself.)

← Old weaving
loom

improved ↑
model

young woman
string weaving

a weaving →
tool. The "even" threads
are moved up and
down

Birch Bark

After endless pounding, birch bark becomes soft enough to make coats and shoes. (These items are also, of course, → stitched together from doe-hair felt or stiff moss fibers.

LEATHER is not readily available. The skin used must come from mice, squirrels, rabbits, or other animals who have died an unnatural death — for example, a car accident, severe frost, pesticides, or fighting.

Leather is also used for making pants, tobacco pouches, boots, shoes, purses, and belts — and sometimes even door hinges.

A few gnomes even own a **silkworm stable** but the silk they gather is mainly used to supply the palace.

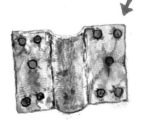

Relations with Animals

Obviously, gnomes maintain close contact with animals. They are, shall we say, on the same wavelength.

This means, of course, that the gnome speaks their language and understands their problems. All animals — even the troublesome ones already mentioned, such as the polecat, rat, etc. — feel safe with the gnome and are trusted by him. The cat, however, remains an exception — especially the wild domestic cat, who is not a member of the natural animal world and is completely unreliable.

Gnomes are often sought out by even such large animals as the wolf, lynx, bear, fox, and wild boar (who are by no means favorites). They know where to find the gnome when they need him. In return, they usually do his bidding without too much sulking.

Some examples of Gnome "First Aid":

Indeed, the gnome is indispensable to the animal world. His intellect and technical skills allow him to do things that animals are incapable of doing themselves.

Foxes and other animals can become irritated by ticks embedded in the skin on their heads or other areas difficult for them to reach. When they try to scrape the tick away against a tree, the insect's head remains under the skin, causing inflammation. The gnome waits until the tick is sleeping, then he twists it out quickly in counterclockwise direction.

When two stags become "entangled" during a fight, that is to say, when their antlers become inextricably entwined (mostly because of extra points or abnormal protrusions), the gnome saws them apart. The poor devils, by then usually half starved, are free once more. Antlers have no feeling, so the whole operation is painless.

When a cow or goat has "the sharps," that is to say, a sharp object lodged in its
paunch (for example, a paring knife it may have swallowed, a piece of glass, or
wire), the gnome will operate to remove it. Normally, the farmer or owner first
discovers the animal's distress and he calls the veterinary; but in neglected
cases or when the owner is too poor to pay the animal doctor, gnomes have
been known to take over.

(The hair on the flank is shaved and the skin opened via a small incision.
The three-layered muscle lining of the abdomen is then pushed open in three
directions and clamped. After the peritoneum has been opened, the side lining
of the stomach becomes visible. After some searching, the sharp object is
located and only a negligible incision is required to remove it. The stomach,
peritoneum, body wall, and skin are stitched up in layers.)

If a rabbit caught in a snare has the presence of mind not to become overexcited and simply to wait patiently, a gnome will soon come along to save him. With a file and pincers, any gnome can manage to lift even the most deeply embedded wire from a rabbit's throat and file it through.

Among other services rendered to rabbits by gnomes, we have already mentioned warnings of impending danger from humans and the wonderful comfort given to rabbits sick with myxomatosis during their last miserable hours.

In addition, gnomes have a way of healing broken limbs (from shotgun or rifle fire or being run over by a car) that is nothing short of miraculous; so much so that one cannot help but suspect the influence of a superior being. Animals wounded in these ways usually withdraw into a thicket for 14 days or so, to allow time for the gnomes to care for them.

Gnomes amuse themselves greatly
by refereeing early-morning
fights between Black cocks

Due to greedy swallowing, acorns and sometimes larger items become lodged in a goose's throat. By using external force with his hands to turn the acorn internally, the gnome helps the nut to glide down into the goose's stomach.

Acupuncture

Gnomes have known about acupuncture for many thousands of years. They use gold and silver needles.

(The badger in the illustration had a perforated cornea, caused by walking into a broken twig in the dark. Needles inserted around the left ear produced anesthesia in the entire left side of its face. When numbness came on, the cornea was stitched in the usual fashion.)

Acupuncture also aids in the removal of deeply imbedded or broken thorns from the paws of animals—a technique as old as the world.

Horses in a stable or meadow will never step on a gnome! (Neither do cows or other large animals.) Without fear, the gnome can walk about between horses' legs or even sleep under them.

Sometimes a deer's antlers become entangled with a piece of wire broken from a fence — or a strand of barbed wire or twisted branch becomes lodged in the antlers. The gnome not only finds this unattractive, but knows that it may cause the deer some danger, and he only too willingly removes the foreign matter.

Squirrels

Squirrels often forget many of the places where they have hidden their nuts for the winter. In long or severe winters this could mean starvation. The gnome of the vicinity, with his infallible memory, will always come to the rescue.

Spiders

Spiders are not especially friends of the gnome; but a gnome will never destroy a web, because that might bring bad luck.

Otters

The gnome makes use of the *otter* to transport him over streams, rivers, or other bodies of water. Swimming and giggling constantly, the otter ferries the gnome to the other side. (Swimming is too risky for gnomes because certain fish are too "fond" of them. True, a gnome could use a bark boat, but these are not at his disposal in every area.)

The old children's rhyme "Ladybug, ladybug, fly away home, Your house is on fire . . .," which makes her actually fly away, originated with gnome children.

The **Mouflon** is a wild sheep imported from Sardinia and Corsica. Because there is often not sufficient stony matter in the moorlands of his new country, his hooves do not wear down as they should and they take on the dimensions of Persian slippers! The gnome saws them off and files them into shape.

The gnome feels the **responsibility** to supply small rodents with food from his storage during the long, severe winter.

Constriction in a deer's chest may be caused by "throat" horseflies. The horsefly lays its eggs in the deer's nose and the larvae work their way into the throat and nestle there. The gnome removes the intruders with a "throat" horsefly pincer.

Throatfly larva actual size

The pincer

A hen pheasant can only count up to three. When she has to cross a ditch with her brood, she waits until the third chick catches up, then continues on her way—leaving the others (who could easily drown) behind her. The gnome helps by finding the abandoned chicks during the twilight hours, locating the mother, and then placing the babes under her.

The gnome does so many favors for wild
boars and deer that they do not begrudge the few
potatoes he takes from the feeding places that farmers
set out for them.

Gnomes have a difficult time accepting polecats because they know that they paralyze living frogs and save them for later eating. The gnome is told about this as a child, and all through his life he has an anxiety that the same fate may await him!

Games

Swinging

Gnome children, like children everywhere, love to swing. There is always a place in the bushes to hang the ropes. In the dunes or meadows, the gnome father builds a swing for them. (Incidentally, adult gnomes like to swing gently when pondering serious problems.)

Gnome children use the **winged seeds** of the maple (Acer pseudoplatanus) to play at being **Dragonflies**

With half of a chestnut husk they pretend to be **Hedgehogs** and frighten the field mice.

Gnome girls like to play with fluffy **willow catkins,** dressing them up as dolls or animals and putting them to bed.

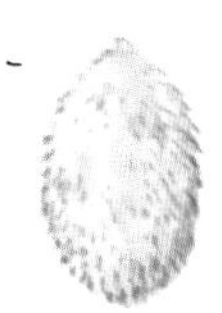

Blowpipes are made from the hollow stems of the flute weed (*Anthriscus vulgaris*) or parsnip (*Pastinaca sativa*).

They play **Marbles** with pebbles or clay balls made by their fathers.
They also play **Territory** – with a pocket knife.
Bowling is played at the edge of a meadow with dried, odorless rabbit droppings; and a respectful audience of rabbits looks on.

Tug of War

Soccer *using a snowberry*

Red rover, Jump rope, Blindman's buff,

Kite flying *(when mother and father aren't looking)* using a Junebug
or bumblebee.
Dressing up *as elves, witches father, mother,*
king, queen, etc.
Balance board
with the most perfect and smoothest boards
Checkers, Flip-the-cap

Authors
Bur-throwing *(to tease animals and*
people)
Gnome parchesi.

<u>Walking on stilts</u> greatly improves the sense of balance

(the stilts measuring up to three feet).

Ice quoits keeps the sense of spacial judgment on the mark.

Through all of this, the gnome has preserved his childlike quality (which also serves to fool trolls).

Making shadows on the wall adds excitement to fairy tales for the children.

Playing games is one way the gnomes keep fit: **tilt at the ring** is not as easy as it looks, and teaches a gnome _dexterity_ in dense undergrowth;

sack-racing is a favorite (and useful);

races for the **advanced** are held in high grass to make it more difficult.

Leapfrog cannot be played sideways because of the pointed caps, and the ♀ have to take their skirts off.

Language

Among themselves gnomes speak their own language. But since we come in contact only with solitary gnomes, we never hear it. (They can become very difficult if asked about their language.) It is certain, however, that animals understand it. "Goodnight" is *slitzweitz*, and "thank you" is *te diews*. We did not progress much beyond these few words mainly because the gnomes master man's languages perfectly. And if they cannot place a word, they immediately ask its meaning. Their written language is the ancient runic script.

"Slitzweitz" = Goodbye

Other Twilight and Night Beings

Elves, Goblins, House Ghosts, Trolls, Dwarfs, River Spirits, Wood Nymphs, Mountain Nymphs, Uldras.

Because the above-mentioned are often confused with gnomes, detailed descriptions follow:

Elves

An elf is an airy spirit of nature, who loves carefree dancing and playing stringed instruments. Elves live underground, or sometimes in or on top of water (preferably a spring), or sometimes even in the air (or in the branches of high trees). Now and then they take on an animal image. They are not malevolent by nature, but sometimes the consequences of their teasing have been serious (for example, causing people to become lost in the marshes) but it is not at all intentional. There are male, female, and sexless elves. Most of them have wings.
Size: from 10 to 30 cm.
Intelligence: sharply focused, but high.

Goblins

Goblins grow to 30 cm. in length; dark little men dressed in black with small pointed caps. They are admittedly malevolent and make no bones about it. When a man dies, they scare his family with their presence, just to be hateful. They are keen on silver and gold and try to wheedle it away from the gnomes. They often carry a small shovel with them. Habitat: only in large stretches of forest, whence they undertake their raids.

goblin
2/3 actual size

House Ghosts

This sort is very often confused with the gnome because they take on many shapes, including that of the gnome—and sometimes also of a rat, cat, or black dog. In their natural state they are invisible to man, but they can become visible in these forms. They make a lot of noise in the house at night; they live between the walls, in the attic or in the cellar, in the stable, in the shed, sometimes even in a large tree beside the house. They are not particularly intelligent, and remain friendly as long as they are treated well. They like to tease lazy people by pulling the blankets off their beds and sending icy drafts through the room. They also delight in knocking over milk pails and keeping people awake by constantly tapping on the walls.

When made very angry, they become malevolent. Their noisemaking becomes unbearable; they throw stones, the cattle become sick, drought or cold weather or continuous storms occur. They leave the house or farm only when it has been totally overwhelmed by disaster and is lost.

Trolls

Distribution area: Norway, Sweden, Finland, Russia, Siberia. Stupid, primitive, distrustful, and unbelievably ugly creatures. They have noses like cucumbers, and a tail. They are horribly strong and fast, and they stink. They often keep boxes full of stolen money and jewels, with which they play for hours, running their fingers through them.
Size: over 1 meter tall.
Hair: black and filthy.

Dwarfs

An almost extinct creature of the male sex. Height 1 meter 20 cm., often smaller. Can still be found in the middle of inhospitable forests and in the mountains. They dig for gold and silver in extensive mines, and live in groups; they are masters of metalwork. They are good-natured except for a solitary few, possibly exiles, who are capable of performing ugly deeds. If a dwarf should fall into human hands, he buys his freedom with gold. They do not have beards.

River Spirits, Wood and Mountain Nymphs

Rarefied, often invisible, beings who can take on any form; they are powerful in the magic arts. Neither good nor ill-natured as such, they avoid all trouble by simply withdrawing. But if they are pushed too far, disasters can occur. They can shed tears in a dismal fashion or laugh lugubriously; often they spy with one eye from behind a tree.

Uldras

Creatures who live underground; to be found only in Lapland. They resemble gnomes but are somewhat larger, and colorless. They live together in large families, or tribes, have authority over big wild animals such as bear, elk, wolf, and reindeer—who obey them completely. They are quite friendly, but blind as bats in the daylight. If they are mistreated by man, disasters may occur. Their ugliest method is to spread a poisonous powder over reindeer moss, causing that animal to die in large numbers and robbing the Lapp herders of their livelihood.

Relations with Other Beings

The gnome doesn't have much to do with elves, goblins, house ghosts, dwarfs, river, wood, or mountain nymphs, uldras, sorcerers, witches or werewolves, fire ghosts or fairies. He simply avoids them.

Gnomes have great difficulty with trolls, however, especially in northern Europe, Russia, and Siberia. These disturbers of the peace—meddlesome and aggressive as they are—cause endless harm to man and animals, with whom the gnome has good relations and toward whom he feels a responsibility.

Fortunately, beyond his cave the troll has no power over the gnome. Besides, the gnome is much more clever. Still, if a troll happens to catch a gnome, the most gruesome things can happen.

A favorite troll pastime is to hold the captured gnome against a revolving grindstone.

Or to hold the gnome so close to a flame that he
fire. He is then thrown from troll to troll—the tr
out the flame with their sweaty hands without
themselves!

Other atrocities: solitary confinement, a knife at the throat, or throwing a knife so that it falls within a hair's breadth of a gnome whose hands and feet are tied. Sometimes the trolls make a gnome dance attached to a chain, or put him on a treadmill—in short, anything a warped mind can think up.

The troll is not malicious enough to want to actually kill the gnome, but in spite of this the gnome sometimes becomes seriously wounded. In almost every case, however, the gnome succeeds in escaping from the troll cave, either through his own ingenuity or with outside help.

Far worse treatment awaits a gnome if he falls into the hands of a snotgurgle, of whom, mercifully, only two or three exist in the world. The snotgurgle is as large as a troll (is perhaps even related to him from primeval times), has six black-clawed fingers on each hand, enormous flat feet with seven toes on each foot. His greasy, stinking body hair is infested with lice and fleas—which seem not to bother him. Hair covers him from head to toe, even on his face, where, between greasy locks, only his gleaming, idiotic eyes can be seen.

Snotgurgles can live to be 2,000 years old, and they are born thieves. In their caves they have huge collections of gold, silver, and precious stones, which they have stolen from men throughout the years. Everything stinks of bugs.

A gnome in the power of a snotgurgle has little chance of survival. There is the case of one Olie Hamerslag (now 385 years old) who resides in the drained marshes near the Berezina. His legs were amputated by a snotgurgle who ran him through a string bean cutting machine. This gnome cunningly succeeded in escaping afterward. He was then flown home by a speckled crow, has used wooden legs for more than seventy years, and now you would hardly know it.

Alas, we also know of a gnome who lost his life: the snotgurgle put him through a mangle. These horrible creatures have also been known to take satanic pleasure, when they discover a gnome dwelling, in lying at the entrance and blowing their foul, scorching breath through the house until all the gnome furniture, irreplaceable portraits, and other cherished possessions have been destroyed. The gnomes, of course, flee through the escape route. But they have to begin their lives all over again elsewhere.

At present, the only snotgurgles to be found are far beyond the Urals, and every gnome within a thousand-kilometer radius is wise enough to give the area a wide berth.

Snotgurgle

The Gnome and the Weather

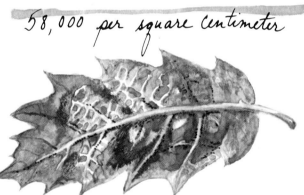

58,000 per square centimeter

Regrettably, we were unable to completely fathom the art of gnome weather forecasting. They do it with an accuracy that any professional weather forecaster would admire. When asked their secret, they mumble vaguely about "feeling it in your bones," indicate that "it just happens," or refer to "old-fashioned know-how," and so on.

We were able to learn, however, that they determine the amount of humidity in the air and the approach of low-pressure systems by the position of the stomata found on the undersides of leaves. An oak leaf has 58,000 stomata per square centimeter. The gnome, with his sharp eyes, is capable of seeing, just by looking at the leaf, if the stomata are open or shut and thus making his calculations—without the aid of computers, of course.

Gnomes also follow closely the 11-year rhythm of sunspots. A third aid comes from studying high-altitude air currents, where changes in weather first occur. This is most probably done with the help of birds.

A great joke of theirs—hoping to lead us astray, no doubt—was to show us what they called the weather tree (*Sertularia cupressina*), which droops in dry weather and revives in humid weather.

Even though the gnome knows exactly what
the weather will be long in advance, he
still goes about in rain, hail, mist, heat,
and cold — weather, after all, does not make
much difference to him.

In severe cold, however, he keeps his hands →
under his beard.

As soon as even one centimeter of ice has formed on lakes, ponds, or puddles, the gnome puts on his skates. If the cold weather continues, skating races are organized.

In thunderstorms the gnome is in little danger of being struck by lightning because he is so small. If the storm really starts to rage, he takes shelter under a beech, because these trees do not attract lightning. Gnomes know the old German rhyme to ward off lightning (the hammer of Thor):

Oak should be avoided,
Don't stand under a willow,
The pine is in danger,
But beech may be safely sought.

Gnomes can forecast a windstorm unerringly, just as animals can. This knowledge is especially important to them—without it they could easily be picked up and blown away.

Snow is also accurately forecast. This is necessary because the gnome uses many openings and holes in the ground, and should these become snowed over, other arrangements would have to be made. (Mention has already been made of the long-distance skis used by gnomes after a snowstorm.)

In the mountains the gnome can predict an avalanche as surely as the chamois, fox, and deer.

The only danger that may befall gnomes in winter, especially in hilly terrain, is that if they are out walking they may get rolled up in a natural snowball as it tumbles down-hill. Many a stunned gnome has been seen picking himself up out of the remains of a snowball that has splattered open against a wall or a mountain chalet!

The Uses of Natural Energy

RATCHET

As simple as it is ingenious!
No noise, no smell.

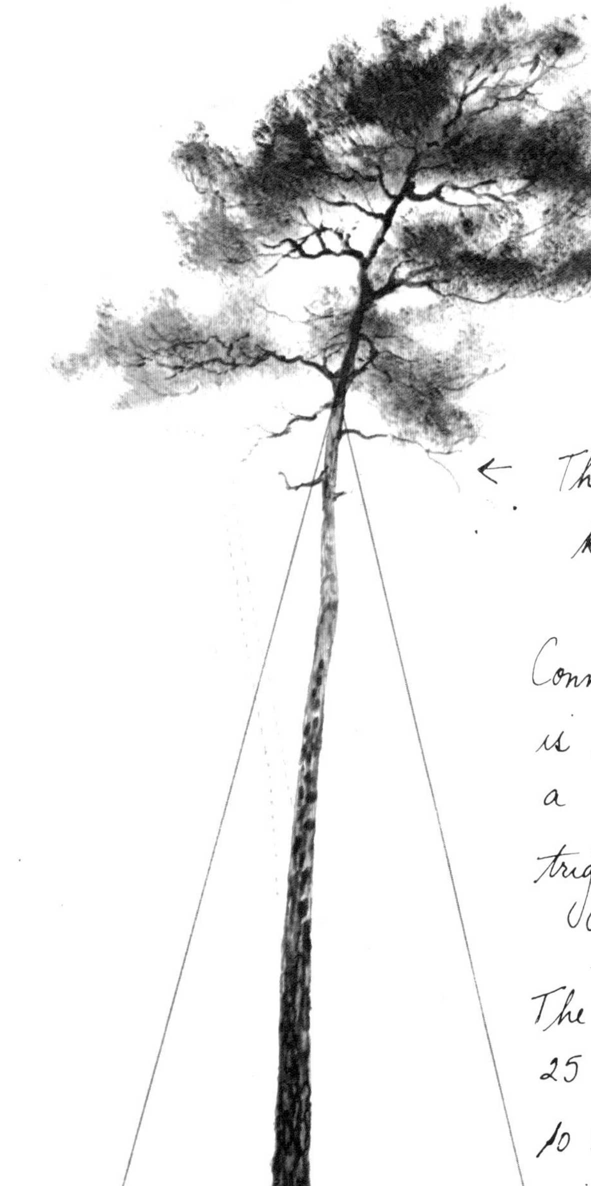

← The tree, waving to and fro,
keeps the ratchet wheel in
constant motion.
Connected to the ratchet wheel
is the hammering machine with
a camshaft that rotates to
trigger the hammers. ↘

The tree is about
25 meters high,
so the pulleys are,
in reality, much smaller
than shown —
about 12 mm
in diameter.

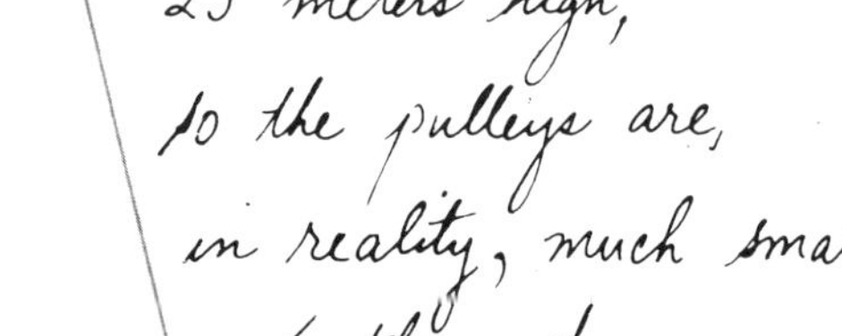

RATCHET WHEEL

CAM

RATCHET WHEEL

PEG WHEEL

FLATTENING HAMMERS
for flattening bark or crushing
oil-filled seeds.

The same method of obtaining energy
    is used for the mill:
grinding corn or acorns,
    beechnuts, etc. —
and for squeezing
    fruit.

RATCHET WHEEL

The Board-sawing machine

As with the hammering machine and the mill, this lumber yard device is situated in thick Blackberry bushes to prevent detection.

Indispensable for house building and gnome industry!

The handsome, smooth boards can only be produced when there is a constant breeze (see Gnome and the Weather)

Tools

double-edged handsaw

pistol-grip handsaw

the large two-man
saw

the sawing
pit

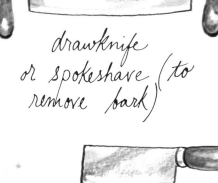

drawknife
or spokeshave (to
remove bark)

woodcarving knives

sickles

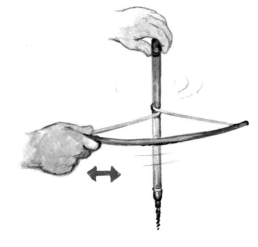

curved drill

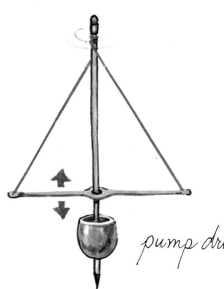

pump drill

shears

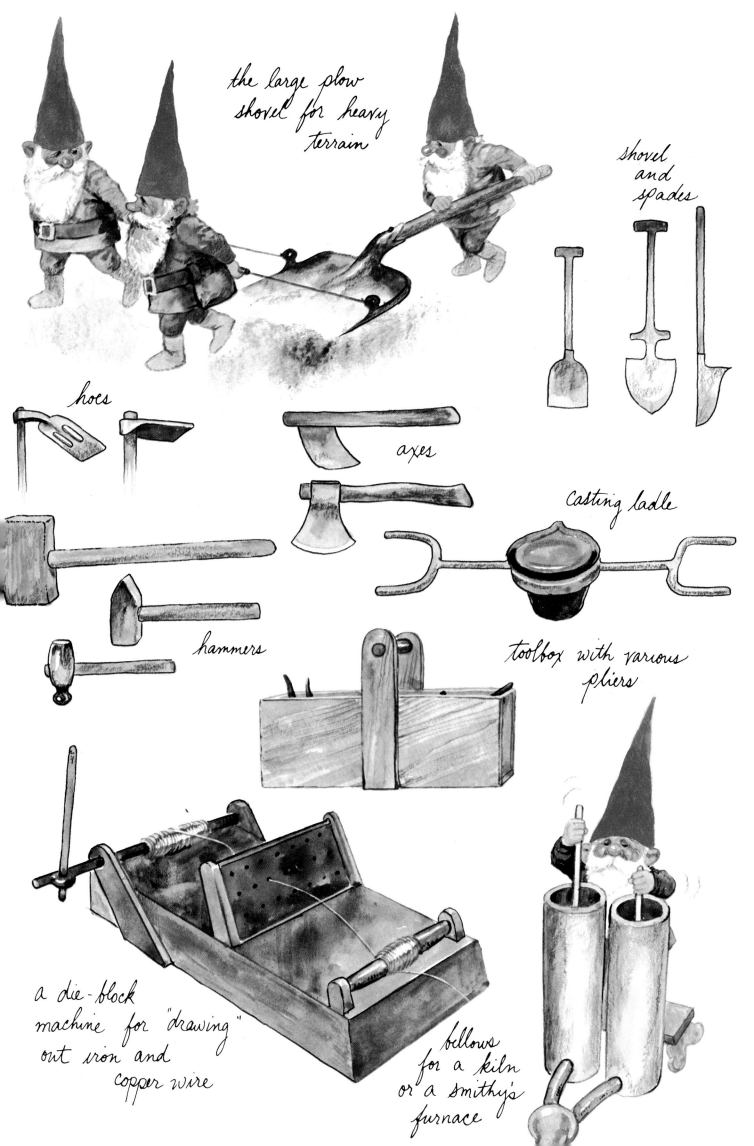

the large plow
shovel for heavy
terrain

shovel
and
spades

hoes

axes

casting ladle

hammers

toolbox with various
pliers

a die-block
machine for "drawing"
out iron and
copper wire

bellows
for a kiln
or a smithy's
furnace

The gnomes construct their water-supply installations in rocky terrain by means of huge drill units (discussed later). They choose two lakes on slightly different levels. When the house has been drilled out they make a vertical passage below it.

Before digging the horizontal passage that is to join the two lakes at a great depth, they sink a tarpaulin in both lakes where the rock drill will strike the lake bed.

The drill bores a passage, first to the lower lake and then to the upper one. As soon as it breaks through the floor of the lake, the tarpaulins are pressed against the floor by suction so that only a small amount of water seeps into the bore holes. The drill is then removed and a pump is placed at the top of the house. At this stage the tarpaulins are removed and the water streams by from high to low. A fine meshed hive is placed over the hole in the upper lake to prevent blockage by mud or sludge. Usually the lakes are clean enough to be used for drinking water. If this is not the case, nitrogen cylinders that extract the dirt and bacteria are installed in the upper passage. These cylinders can be changed by means of an ordinary diving bell that the gnomes use for their other lake bed investigations. The constant stream ensures fresh water.

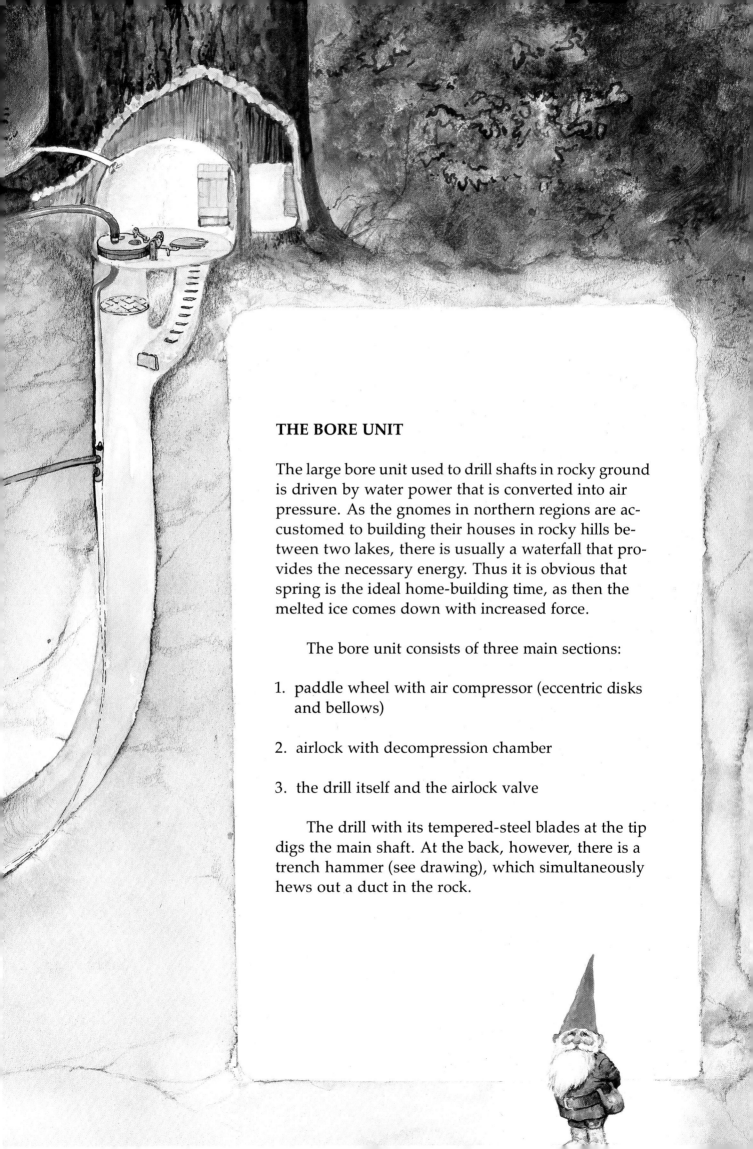

THE BORE UNIT

The large bore unit used to drill shafts in rocky ground is driven by water power that is converted into air pressure. As the gnomes in northern regions are accustomed to building their houses in rocky hills between two lakes, there is usually a waterfall that provides the necessary energy. Thus it is obvious that spring is the ideal home-building time, as then the melted ice comes down with increased force.

The bore unit consists of three main sections:

1. paddle wheel with air compressor (eccentric disks and bellows)

2. airlock with decompression chamber

3. the drill itself and the airlock valve

The drill with its tempered-steel blades at the tip digs the main shaft. At the back, however, there is a trench hammer (see drawing), which simultaneously hews out a duct in the rock.

AIR COMPRESSOR

By means of a paddle wheel at the foot of a waterfall, the water energy is transferred to the camshaft with eccentric disks (A), and thence by way of the propelling rods (B), onto the yokes (C), which are connected to each other by a common shaft (D). The yokes move the membranes of the bellows (E) up and down, thus producing air pressure without any pollution. This can only be achieved by using the one-way air passage suction valve holes. (The development of this mechanism probably led to the creation of the *Rommelpot,* an old, western European musical instrument made of a jug and a pig's bladder.)

The air compressed in the bellows goes via the air pipe (G) and the second hole (N2) of the wooden distributor (see Airlock) to the large bore shaft, resulting in high atmospheric pressure while work is in progress.

AIRLOCK WITH DECOMPRESSION CHAMBER

In the airlock there is a wooden distributor (H) with holes N1 and N2, which can be maneuvered by means of the cogged bar (M). When at rest the air goes through opening N1, when in operation through opening N2. The illustration shows it at rest. To keep the pressure in the lock constant, a regulating valve (K) has been introduced. Next to the lock chamber is a decompression chamber (L) by which the gnomes enter and leave. The adjustable sliding scuttle (J) is situated in the channel or duct, and this enables the grit to be removed to the outside under the waterfall.

In the duct next to the main shaft is a rope (green) connected to a bell in the lock chamber that allows the gnomes to sound an alarm or simply signal a request to be pulled up for food or to sign off for the day.

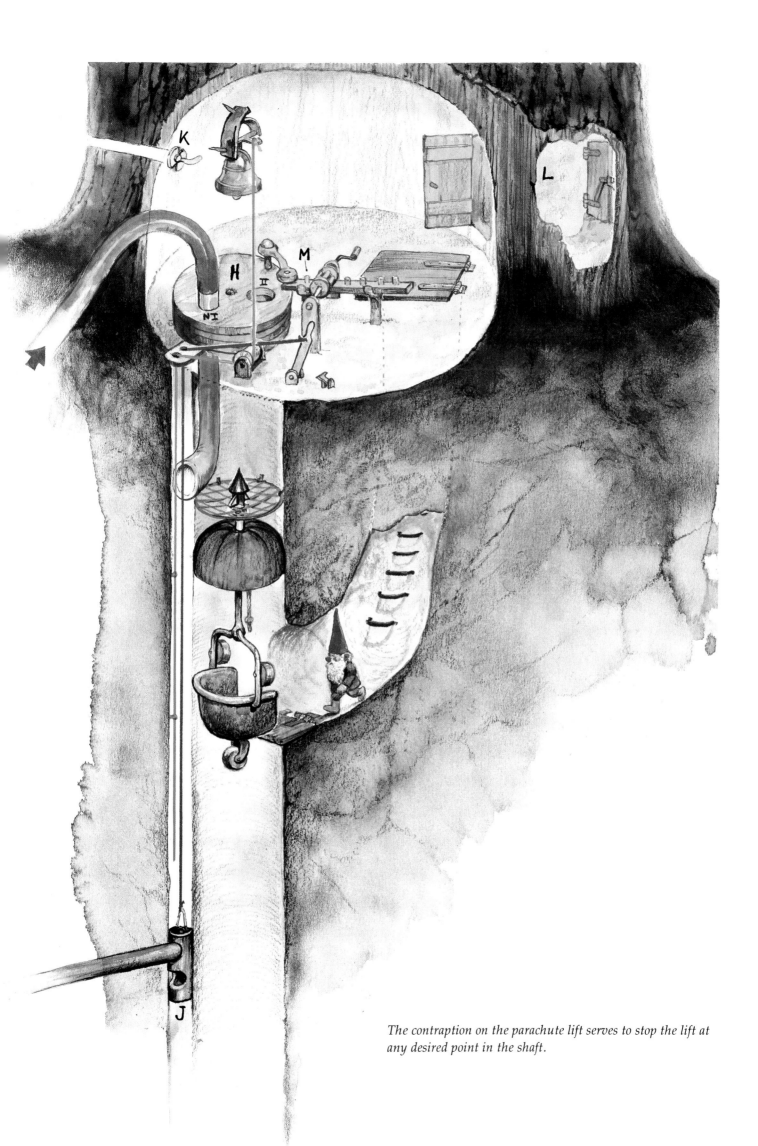

The contraption on the parachute lift serves to stop the lift at any desired point in the shaft.

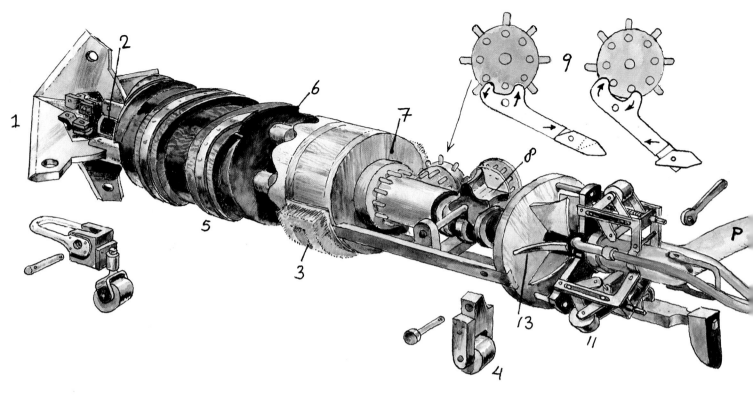

DRILLING MACHINE

The tempered-steel blades (1) do the actual digging and hewing. The effective cooling of the waste compressed air prevents their becoming overheated. The grit loosened by the blades is removed via the upper suction channel (2) and the lower, brush-lined suction channel (3) to the pipe (P) and then via the duct to the scuttle (J) outside. When not in use, the drill can be moved on the coasters (4). After the preliminary work of the tempered-steel blades, the walls of the main shaft are smoothed by walnut rollers with steel grinding strips (5).

The hammer cogs (6) get the power from the cam unit (7). The shape of the cam unit causes a revolving hammer motion to the hammer cogs, turning the entire foremost part of the drill and resulting in the notching stroke of the blades. In order to reduce the revolutions, thus increasing the power of the blades, cog-wheel-reduction is applied (8). The drill is pushed slowly forward during drilling with the help of the creeping cog (9).

Naturally the energy for all this is obtained from the compressed air, which is conveyed through the red jet tubing previously mentioned (10) or (O) to make the propeller (13) rotate, which in turn passes the revolving motion forward by means of a corkscrew shaft. The insertion wheel (11) is added to make underground bends negotiable.

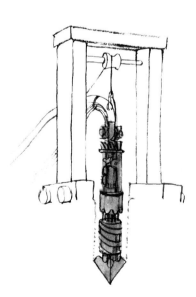

LOCK DOOR

The round, barrel-shaped lock door is situated under the main shaft. A normal rectangular door is built into it. The high pressure in the main shaft passes through the lock by means of the three red jet tubes of the compressed air supply (O), which is then conducted to the actual bore units. The turnvalve (Q) serves to shut off the shaft or duct.

While the rectangular door in the round lock door remains closed, the compressed air is forced to find its way through the red tubes (O). If the door is opened the pressure in the tubes disappears and the machine stops. Back through the lock door goes the tube for grit removal

(P), which connects by means of a bayonet mount (R) with the side duct. This duct is covered over with duct-covering planks (S). The grit is removed by the spent pressure in reverse from the machine and is conducted back via the channel (P).

To prevent the lock door from slipping off into the depths during vertical drilling, the expansion bar contraption (T) has been invented, by means of which the whole lock door can be jammed in the curve of the shaft wall.

This is how the situation can be at any given moment: the parachute lift is at the bottom of the shaft just behind the round lock door. The drill is working at full capacity.

The grit is being removed via the duct and the scuttle and is taken outside.

The midnight break arrives, and the gnomes down below want to come up. They open the rectangular door that cuts off the air pressure from the machine, causing it to stop. Then they lift up a duct plank and pull on the rope that jingles the bell up above. The plank is then replaced.

The gnome engineer above turns the distributor with the cog bar so that the compressed air no longer gets into the main shaft but goes via the hole N1 into the duct. At the same time he lowers the scuttle so that the compressed air does not escape through the gravel-removal tube, but goes straight down and blows the whole duct clean. This air reverses at the bottom of the shaft and comes up via the main shaft, blowing the parachute lift up in front of it. Alas, this is not done without creating a cloud of dust that fortunately does not last long. The gnomes get out, climb the ladder to the air lock, and leave their work site via the decompression chamber.

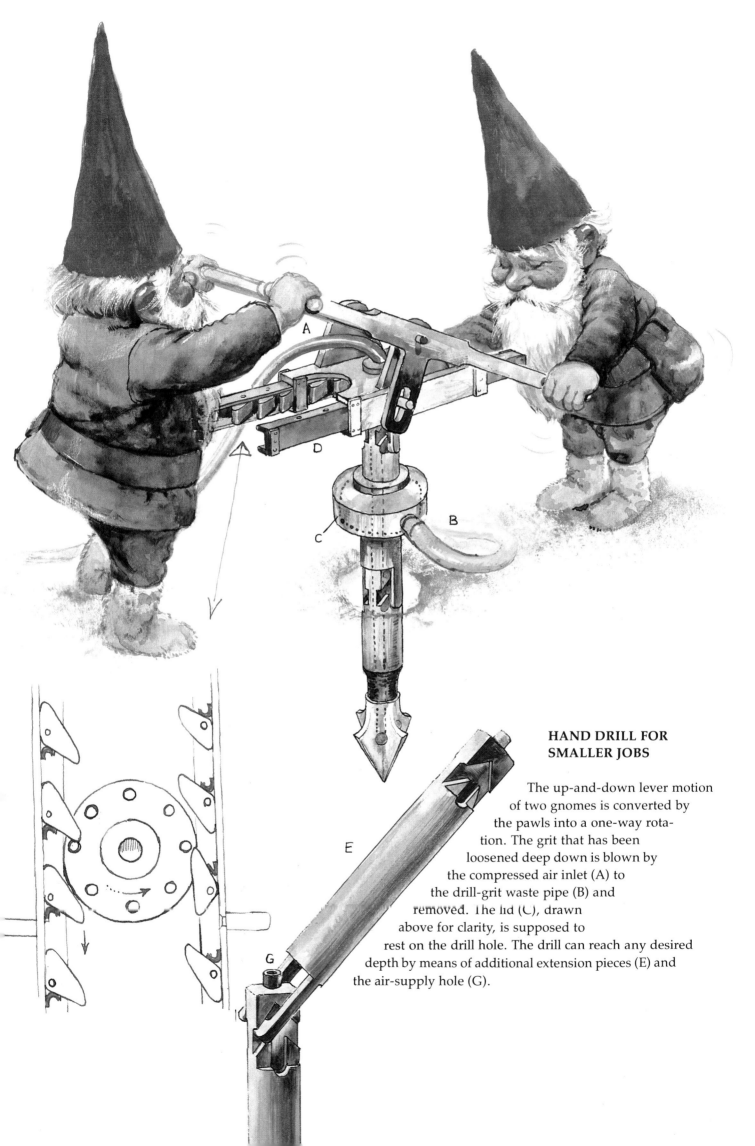

HAND DRILL FOR SMALLER JOBS

The up-and-down lever motion of two gnomes is converted by the pawls into a one-way rotation. The grit that has been loosened deep down is blown by the compressed air inlet (A) to the drill-grit waste pipe (B) and removed. The lid (C), drawn above for clarity, is supposed to rest on the drill hole. The drill can reach any desired depth by means of additional extension pieces (E) and the air-supply hole (G).

CAVE ENLARGER

The cave enlarger is an axle to which chains with iron
balls are attached; a rotating motion causes a
formidable bombardment of the rock face.
The gnomes make little of the seeming
labor hazards of this machine.

The construction of the interior
of the rocky hollow begins after all
the drilling has been done and the
unit has been collected above ground by the contractor.
The wood for the house is loosely positioned
<u>outside</u> so that it can be permanently assembled
within.

First, however, the tarpaulins
are withdrawn from the drill
holes and pulled up so that the water can
flow freely between the lakes

Gnomes know exactly where Mother Nature can spare a tree... —

and how to hew it.

first wedge

fall wedge

For an ax to be wieldable it should reach from the ground to the navel (this does not apply to humans).

To obtain a straight surface on the trunk, a chalked string is pulled taut lengthwise. By pulling up the string and letting it snap back, a neat chalk line is made that indicates where the gnome must cut. →

He uses an ordinary ax for the rough profile.

As side straighteners, adz and

drawknife are used. →

Father and son help each other saw the trunk to size.

From time to time the teeth have to be pushed outward with a saw set.

For the so-called semicircular joint, the trunk is sawed to different depths and the curve is chiseled out.

Pulleys are favored for transporting wood.

The ornamental rods are turned by means of a swaying Larix branch.

He does the sawing and notching to size of
the biggest logs where the trees are felled
(usually near his parents' house).

Then he transports them,
gliding →
← pulling
or
floating.
↓

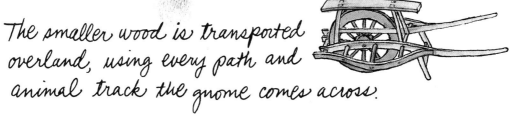

The smaller wood is transported overland, using every path and animal track the gnome comes across.

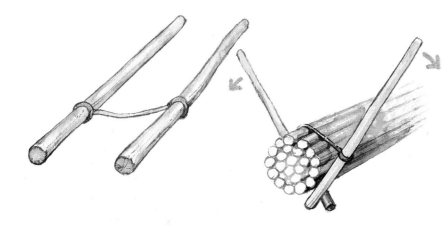

Fine poles are tied in a bundle, the so- called marling hitch.

When the building material arrives at the site of the house-to-be, the gnome pulls it in immediately so he can insert a revolving door (edged with brushes of the woolly rhinoceros)

in order to keep out undesirables (like vipers).

To begin with, he puts out a couple of squatters.

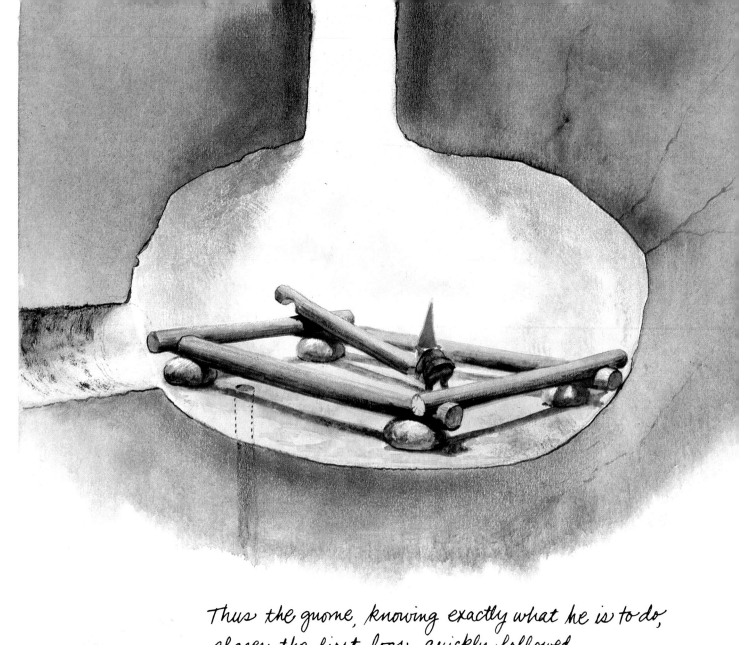

Thus the gnome, knowing exactly what he is to do,
places the first logs, quickly followed
by the masonry for oven,
air,
and
smoke flues.

beer offered
to the →
house
builders

The Housewarming Party

A bride is not allowed to see the new house before her marriage.
The parents of the bride and groom inspect the house when it is
ready. The bride's father brings a wine-colored chest under his
arm that he does not hand over until he has conducted a
thorough inspection of the locks, masonry, carpentry products,
the quality of the furnishings, etc.,
and has found them to his liking.
The chest contains earth from the
immediate surroundings of the
bride's home. If the father of the
bride is satisfied with everything,
the chest is cemented into one of
the walls and the deal is clinched.

THE EMOTIONAL LIFE OF THE GNOME

A gnome is so close to nature that he is always making friends and acquaintances, which must be very pleasant. He likes everything and everybody. He is used to giving. He doesn't ask for what he gets as a matter of course, such as love, affection, or material things. A gnome knows no fear, but is precautious and knows when to get out of the way. He has an inborn feeling of security. This is hereditary, but is, to no mean degree, strengthened by the way his mother enfolds him from the time of his birth, namely by the completely natural use of cuddle circles.

Here are some examples of cuddle circles that exert a positive influence throughout the entire life of a gnome.

It is by no means limited to only mother-child relationships; father-child or other combinations are just as good!

It's easy to sum up: just as much love and tenderness as is poured into a child is returned to others throughout his life. A feeling of security and of being one with earth and cosmos results in the so-called cosmic-telluric attachment, which is seldom found in humans. It has nothing to do with being brave or not brave—quite the contrary: because gnomes operate from a safe basis, their physical and mental capacity is at a maximum. They never panic. Just as other beings, the gnome must have developed his emotions via his sense of touch.

TOUCH
From birth the sense of touch is responsible for the first observations, awareness, and knowledge. All other senses have evolved

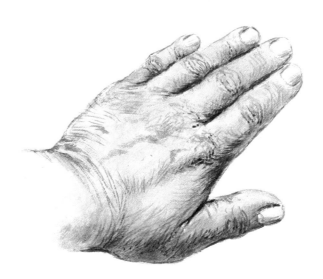

from this one. It is very stupid to answer a child's enquiry "What is that?" with "That is for leaving alone." A child has to have an object in his hands to know for the rest of his life what the object really represents.

Touch is thus the organ of knowledge. Touch lies in the wrapping of the body—the skin. The mouth is extremely important to children for touching and discovering purposes. In the beginning touch transmits messages that are registered and catalogued within. As feelings and emotions are built up over the years, touch no longer only receives but also gives out sympathy, comfort, tenderness, and love.

THE HAND
To beings blessed with reason, the hand is the ideal instrument with which to feel. A maximum of touch qualities and expressive possibilities are centered in the hands, and it is a part of the body with inconceivable versatility. Moreover, gesticulations and the offering and shaking of a hand nearly always have an emotional meaning.

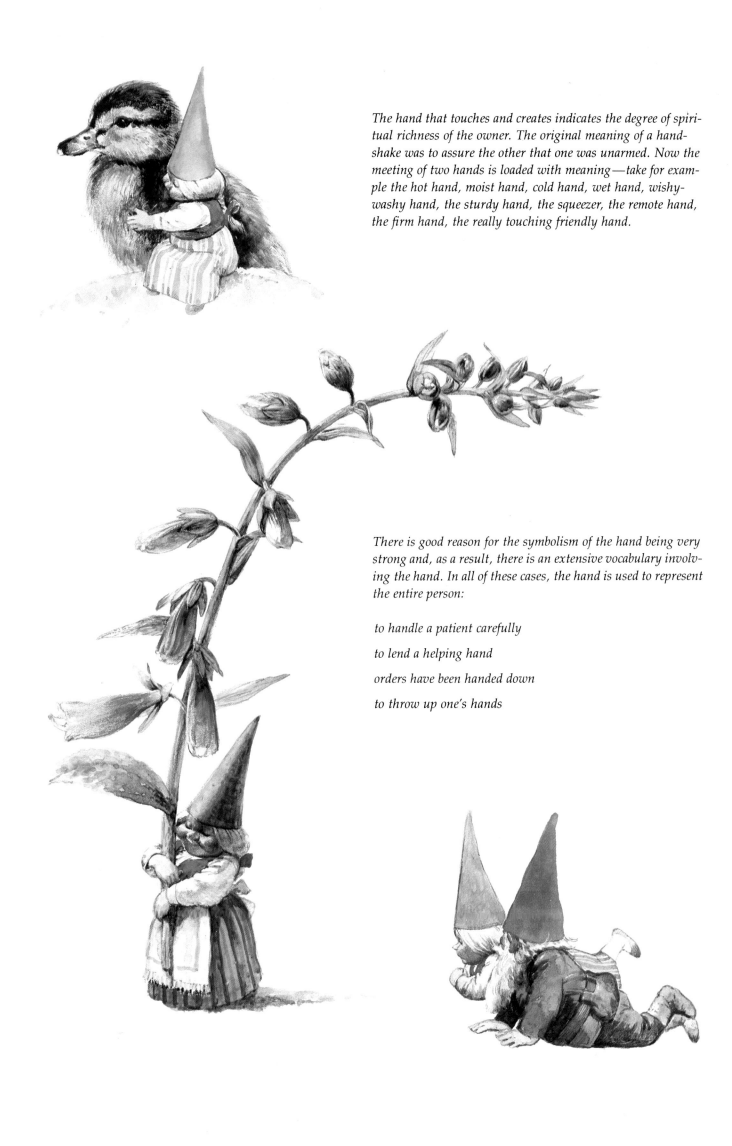

The hand that touches and creates indicates the degree of spiritual richness of the owner. The original meaning of a handshake was to assure the other that one was unarmed. Now the meeting of two hands is loaded with meaning—take for example the hot hand, moist hand, cold hand, wet hand, wishy-washy hand, the sturdy hand, the squeezer, the remote hand, the firm hand, the really touching friendly hand.

There is good reason for the symbolism of the hand being very strong and, as a result, there is an extensive vocabulary involving the hand. In all of these cases, the hand is used to represent the entire person:

to handle a patient carefully

to lend a helping hand

orders have been handed down

to throw up one's hands

The hand can also be strongly symbolic on its own:

an imploring hand

a blessing hand

a conjuring hand

the laying on of a healing hand

the handshake to seal the contract

a greeting hand

the extended hand

the protecting hand

with a rough hand

with a gentle hand

a searching or probing hand

with folded hands

the life-giving hand

Gnomes pat the trunks of trees and say "Hello brother tree," just as we pat a dog or the nose of a horse. (He does that too to any old animal.) From tenderness, love comes naturally. This applies to everything.*

* Refer to I. Corinthians 13:4–7.

TENDERNESS

Tenderness means—and imparts—warmth and respect. The whole hand expresses the quality of the meeting, not just the fingers, which express feeling without depth. Only the whole hand can encircle something tenderly. A small child (one who is frightened, for example) must be lifted by the encircling hands of someone squatting. This conveys a feeling of warmth and safety to the child. WRONG is: lifting while standing upright and leaning stiffly forward. Here the hand circumvention is missing and the high/low feeling is increased instead of reduced. A tender hand always gives, never takes. A caressing hand entices and takes. It has only sexual significance.

The harmony of nature has become so much a part of the gnomes that they can't make head nor tail of human aggression and cruelty. The Iron Curtain means nothing, nor does war, fratricide, theft, envy, struggle for power, or any other human misery. Should the backwash of human cruelty touch them directly, they simply step aside.

DISUNITY

Differences of opinion, irritation, and minor quarrels naturally do occur from time to time in gnome marriages. The usual solution is for the grieved party to sing the complaint in a self-made song, whereupon the guilty party usually starts laughing and acknowledges that he or she has been wrong.

If this fails, it becomes more serious. This method is then tried: for a solid fifteen minutes wife tells husband what she thinks of him. Husband may only answer the next day, when he will get equal time, and so forth. This usually solves everything.

Many a quarrel ends in a pleasant bath.

While the gnome boys are away from home copying the Secret Book, gnome girls are busy learning too. The girls learn how to handle all sorts of wounds and bone fractures in the veterinary hospital.

In the game reserves for threatened animal species nearly all the helpers are female gnomes. In the Bat Reserve near Ede, in Holland, for example, it is common knowledge that gnome women have been taken on as maternity and parasite specialists.

Patching the colors of damaged butterflies requires artistic craftsmanship.

Another life's work of female gnomes is the creation and up-keep of subterranean fishponds. These are huge grottoes containing lakes that are either natural or hewn into the rocks. Into the steep cliffsides around the lake, paths are chiseled out where lanterns and torches are hung. There are grottoes that narrow to small openings behind which new lakes can be found, even numbering as many as twelve, which is a fantastic sight in the flaring torchlight.

All fishes from prehistoric times up till today are preserved in these subterranean lakes. Some have phosphorescent bodies with all the colors of the rainbow; others have lighted fins and tails; still others have eyes like torches. All salt- and fresh-water fishes are represented, including deep sea fishes. Controlling the oxygen supply in seawater is quite a job.

If any species on earth is threatened with extinction it is extra specially cared for here.

The biggest and most complete fishponds are under the Ural Mountains· Huge underground waters also used for this purpose are under the Ardennes; in Norway; in the Balkans; and in the Rocky Mountains.

Legends of the Gnomes

1

In a small house in the middle of a dark, sprawling forest lived a poor woodsman.

He had a wife, six children, and a black cat with one eye who kept the rats and mice at bay. The children had to walk two hours to get to school. Beside the little house was a vegetable garden and even a little flower garden; in the barn were two skinny goats and a pig.

But the family could hardly manage on the meager earnings of a woodsman, even though the father left the house before dawn and arrived home—exhausted—long after sunset. Though they had plenty of firewood and a clear stream nearby, the wife often sighed to her husband:

''How can we possibly bring up all our children?''

And the woodsman would shrug his shoulders and say he couldn't work any harder than he already did, and this was true.

One day as he was arriving home in the twilight he saw in the distance the cat leaving the woods with a rat in its mouth. But something was strange: the rat had no tail. Filled with curiosity, the woodsman approached the cat who was sitting under a bush. She hissed malevolently as he came closer, but the woodsman wasn't afraid. He grabbed the cat by the base of her tail with one hand and with the other pressed against her jaws until she opened her mouth and let the thing fall.

''Well, I'll be,'' said the woodsman. Because what he had picked up was not a rat, but a gnome woman. She was dead.

The woodsman had seen a gnome once, but never a female one. He took her inside and wiped away a few drops of blood on her cheeks and legs. His wife and children stroked the doll-like little being and laid her on the window seat in the living room while they ate their

meal of potatoes and bacon fat in the kitchen. When they came back, the little gnome woman was gone.

"Maybe the cat has got her again," the wife said, but the cat still sat sulking under the bush outside, showing one angry eye. The family gave up searching and went to bed, as everyone had to be up early in the morning.

The woodsman woke up in the middle of the night. Something was tugging gently at his ear. Beside his head stood a gnome. "You saved my wife," he said. "What can I do to reward you?" "But she was dead, wasn't she?" the woodsman asked, sleepily. "She was only pretending to be dead. Luckily, she's still full of life—oh, a scratch here, a few black-and-blue marks there—but she'll get over it. Just tell me what you want as a reward. Here is a little flute. When you blow on it, I'll return." And just like that—he disappeared!

The woodsman and his wife discussed the matter the rest of the night. They finally decided to ask if they might have three wishes, just as in the fairy tales.

The following evening the woodsman blew on the flute, and shortly thereafter the gnome appeared.

"I'd like to have three wishes," said the woodsman, somewhat timidly, while his wife poked at the fire behind him.

The gnome looked a little glum but finally said:

"Well, go on then—what is your first wish?"

"I want a nugget of gold so I won't have money worries anymore."

The gnome shook his head.

"You can have it, but gold seldom brings happiness."

"I don't care," said the woodsman.

"And the other two wishes?"

"We haven't decided yet."

"Well, just blow on the flute when you want me again," said the gnome with a sigh.

Next morning, there on the front steps of the little house lay a gold nugget as big as an orange, sparkling in the sun. The woodsman grabbed it up and yelled, "We're rich, we're rich!" And then he carried the nugget to the village to exchange it for money. But no one in the village had ever seen a gold nugget before and no one knew what it was worth. The blacksmith advised the woodsman to take it to a jeweler in the city. The woodsman set off at once; but instead of going the long way he took a shortcut through the swamps that he remembered from the days of his youth. As he danced along the way, admiring his gold nugget, he slipped off the path and plunged into a quagmire and immediately began to sink. He tried to reach out for firm ground, but couldn't make it. In one hand he clutched the gold nugget, and with the other he struggled to get the flute out of his pocket so that he could signal the gnome. He was barely able to reach it and blow a shrill blast.

He had sunk up to his neck in mud when the gnome appeared.

"Get me out of here," cried the woodsman.

"That is your second wish," said the gnome. He then stuck two fingers in his mouth and whistled shrilly—and in a few minutes he was surrounded by six other gnomes. Using their little axes, the gnomes chopped down a nearby tree so that it fell across the quagmire right next to the woodsman. He was able to hoist himself up onto it and get back to the path from which he had fallen. When he looked around, the gnomes had disappeared.

But still he had the gold nugget in his hand. He went on his way, muddy and shivering; eventually, his clothes dried and his courage returned. He found a jeweler in the city and entered his shop. The jeweler was a distinguished-looking man in a white smock; he wore gold-rimmed glasses. Frowning at the enormous nugget of gold and at the woodsman's bedraggled appearance, the jeweler weighed the nugget. Then he asked the woodsman to wait a few minutes and scurried out of his shop through the back door to notify the police. A half hour later the woodsman found himself in the police station.

"And now tell us where you stole this gold," said a fat police sergeant in a fatherly fashion.

The commissioner of police asked the same question an hour later—but in a less fatherly fashion.

"I didn't steal it," cried the woodsman in despair, "I got it from a gnome."

"Of course, from a gnome," said the commissioner, who had never seen a gnome—and *would* never, because he was such an unpleasant person. "Not even one grain of gold has ever been found in this country in a thousand years—but that doesn't occur to this gentleman, does it? Lock him up!"

During the days that followed, the woodsman was questioned again and again—and threatened with dire consequences if he did not reveal the source of the gold. Finally, he was examined by a doctor, but even he could cast no light on the matter except to report that the woodsman kept babbling away about gnomes.

None of these people had ever seen a gnome because they all had ugly souls.

Meanwhile, the gold nugget was kept in the vault of the city council. After a week went by, the woodsman became so miserable that, one night, he blew the flute. After two hours, the gnome appeared.

"My wife and children are starving," the woodsman said. "I want to get out."

"That is your third wish," replied the gnome, "but I have already taken care of your wife and children." The gnome went that same night to consult a lawyer in the city who had a house gnome. Next day, the lawyer visited the police and succeeded in having the woodsman freed, owing to lack of evidence. But the gold remained behind for safekeeping until its theft could be verified.

The woodsman gladly went back to his work. The forest had never seemed so spacious and free as it did after his stay in the stuffy cell in the city; he was happy and satisfied—even though he often thought of the gold.

From that time on, things improved for him in all sorts of ways. First, a rich foreigner bought all the logs the woodsman had cut for twice the usual price. Next, the same man asked if the woodsman would become his overseer.

The happy woodsman was given a cheerful house at the edge of a village, and close to the school. He earned much more than before and his troubles were over.

A few months later he came across the gnome in the woods.

"And?" the gnome asked, "Have you got your gold back yet?"

"Not yet," the woodsman said, "It seems to be a criminal act in this country to possess gold. But even without it, my troubles are over."

"So, there you are," the gnome said—and disappeared into the bushes.

Legends of the Gnomes

2

In among the dark, warm beams of a windmill in northern Holland lived a gnome family. The miller knew them well. He had once saved the gnome wife from being crushed by the millstone. The miller always set aside milk and cornmeal for the gnome family. In exchange, they kept a watch out for fires, and warned him of coming storms or windy weather. The miller was thus always able to tie back the sails of his windmill's arms in time to prevent them from rotating wildly and possibly causing a fire due to the friction—a common hazard of windmills.

If a member of the miller's family became ill, the gnome came to call and laid his tiny, wrinkled hand on the fevered brow; he also left behind powerful medicinal herbs. This treatment usually resulted in a quick recovery.

In short, all was well in the windmill, not only physically but also financially. The miller and his wife were hardworking and intelligent and they had pleasant children.

But nearby lived some lazy folk who were less intelligent and whose wives had too free a hand with money. Envious, these vicious neighbors spread the rumor that the miller dabbled in black magic and that this was the reason for his great prosperity. Most people took no notice of these whisperings, but among the malcontents the rumors persisted.

In one of these dens of gossip lived a bright eleven-year-old girl with straw-blond braids. It was hard

to believe that she could be the daughter of such stupid and narrow-minded parents—but this sometimes happens. She knew all there was to know about animals and plants and was wonderfully gifted at modeling clay. A sweet and patient girl, one could tell that she would grow up to be a beauty. She had heard all the stories going around the village, and it became obvious to her that the miller's prosperity was due to gnomes living in the mill and not to black magic. She would have given anything to have had a gnome of her own, but because of her parents they always passed her house by.

One day at school she modeled a lifelike gnome in clay with the help of her teacher. The neighborhood potter was kind enough to fire the modeled gnome in his kiln. Afterward, the girl painted the gnome's cap blue (incorrectly, of course), his blouse red, and his pants and boots green. She also fashioned a little wooden

wheelbarrow and placed the statue with it among the flowers in her parents' garden.

Her parents made fun of the statue, but they did not remove it. The gnomes in the mill heard of it, of course, and came to look at it. They were touched. As a reward they brought a present for the girl every month. And her sweetness and determination had such a good influence as the years went by that her parents became less backward and more generous. As a result—and with a certain amount of luck—they became more prosperous.

But the remaining dullards naturally misunderstood all this and muttered among themselves: "If you have a gnome statue in your garden you will become rich."

Absolute nonsense, of course. But such ideas catch on. And ever since, it has been a tradition in some homes to have a gnome—with or without a wheelbarrow—in the garden.

Legends of the Gnomes

3

The farm stood on a mound beside a seemingly endless dyke. Farther on, to the south of the river, there was nothing but vast reed- and grassland, dotted with small pools. Beyond, there was only stark loneliness, as far as the eye could see.

There were many hares, partridges, curlews, pheasants, oyster catchers, black-tailed godwits, geese, teal, swans, coots, and even otters. A gnome family lived in the roof of the farmhouse.

When winter began, the father gnome and his two 80-year-old sons warned the hares of impending high water and advised them to move. But the hares simply stared with large silly eyes, took no notice of the advice, and continued their carefree running about, chasing female hares and preening their ears.

The water began to rise at the end of February. It rained day after day, and the people living upstream were forced to build a spillway into the reed- and grassland. Cork-dry reeds and blackberry brambles were deluged overnight. The young hares were the first to drown. All

winged creatures sought safety. The adult hares were driven back onto the high ground, but as these areas too disappeared under water, the hares panicked and drowned—needlessly, for hares, like all four-footed animals, are excellent swimmers.

Finally, the plain was transformed into a large watery mirror, with here and there only a tree top, a few reed plumes, and tops of bushes to be seen. The water continued to rise.

An area of high ground not far from the dyke called the Broomstick (witches were supposed to have lived there in the old days) became the refuge for the last 8 hares to survive out of 200. But there was no shelter from the icy winds or the eyes of beasts of prey.

Water birds notified the gnomes of the hares' plight.

But the gnomes realized that they couldn't count on any human assistance because there was an unsympathetic farm worker nearby with a hunting rifle.

That evening the gnomes were fortunate enough to see the wooden gate of a picket fence floating by. The water was level with the dyke, so they lashed the gate as best they could to the land. Cleverly, they increased its buoyancy by binding loose beams and driftwood beneath it, and at about 3:00 A.M. it rose high enough out of the water to bear considerable weight.

The gnomes dragged the raft to a point where the hard northwester blew directly toward the hares' island; they jumped aboard and let the wind carry them. It was bitterly cold on the bare raft and they felt very lonely amid the dark, turbulent elements. To keep warm—and to speed up the slow-floating raft—they rowed a bit with a loose plank.

Two and a half hours later they reached the Broomstick. The hares were wet, hungry, and nervous. They ran skittishly about, stamping their hindfeet. So frightened were they that they dared not approach the raft. Whenever one would put a foot on the raft, he would pull back, run to the other side of the island, and sit huddled up and shivering.

All the while, it rained continuously and the wind sent showers of foam over animal and gnome alike.

Finally, the father gnome warned the hares in a booming voice that within two hours at most the Broomstick would be under water. They had better make haste. That got them going at last! First on board was an old mother; she was followed by the others, a tick-ridden male hare bringing up the rear.

The gnomes found it impossible to row the heavily laden raft against the wind, for in the meantime the northwester had taken on storm proportions. All they could do was to drag the raft to the other side of the island and let the wind take them. They hoped they would reach land somewhere. It was an uncertain plan, but the only one that could be carried out. The hares offered no help. They sat rolling their eyes, numbed with fear.

Fortunately, the raft proceeded with more speed than before because of the heightened storm and the eight wind-catching hare bodies on board.

The Broomstick disappeared slowly from sight. Across the water beyond the island the twinkling lights of the farmhouse, where it was safe and warm, became smaller and smaller. All around lay endless black water and curling crests of waves. The wind wailed.

The gnomes stood together and, with troubled eyes, searched a horizon that had melted into one dark mass. Everyone was soaking wet and freezing cold.

Hours later, as it began to get light, land suddenly loomed up in front of them. The raft ran aground on the edge of a new dyke road under construction. It was a wide, safe wall of sand disappearing in both directions into the lonely distance, but with lots of grass and weeds growing on it. The hares skipped off the raft, relieved, and stiffly ran away, stopping now and then to take in the new terrain with their large, frightened eyes, but never turning back with a ''fare thee well'' or a ''thank you.''

The gnomes consulted the secret maps that they had brought and planned their return route to the farm. The journey would have to be undertaken in daylight, because there was no shelter or gnome house in which to hide.

No one, however, saw the little men as they hurried forth on their long hike, not even as they crept past farms and houses—mainly because they have special techniques for this. Fortunately, too, there were still low-hanging dark clouds in the sky, and it rained at times.

By afternoon they reached home; they ate a huge meal and slept for twelve hours under the most comfortable blankets in the world.

Legends of the Gnomes

4

In Kharkov, people enjoy telling this story. Just outside their town lived a certain Tatjana Kirillovna Roeslanova. She was seventy years old but still had a pretty, straight nose and shining white hair which she parted in the middle. She had been exiled from Moscow by the secret police; her husband was dead and she was without resources. Nobody was allowed to employ her, so to make a livelihood she bought a cow with money from secret friends.

Then she did something that Soviet authorities prefer not to see, but tolerate through necessity. She supplied ten houses on the outskirts of the town with milk—they would, otherwise, have had to travel so far for their milk that it would no longer be fresh when they returned. Tatjana lived in a shack in the middle of a small

vegetable garden and spent the days grazing her cow along the roadside.

There are hundreds of thousands of these one-cow businesses in Russia. The economic consequences of removing them would be so great that the government turns a blind eye.

And so Tatjana grazed her cow by day, was continually affectionate to her, and at night brought her into a corner of the shack for milking. In the opposite corner of the shack, behind a black cloth, a number of religious icons were hidden. Tatjana had managed to smuggle them from her large Moscow house, and daily she prayed before them. The cow gave 20 liters of milk a day; but there was a six-week dry period when she was expecting her calf (every year she was sent to a bull owned by a sympathetic farmer) and Tatjana had to reckon on this period in stretching her earnings over the entire year.

Although Tatjana had once been a well-to-do lady, she accepted her lot and made the best of it. She always sought out new roads, searching for the best grass for her cow, but usually returned home through the same dense alder thicket not far from her shack. In the center of the wood were a few large boulders. Under the boulders lived two gnome families with nearly adult children. Every day Tatjana stopped in the woods and picked up from under a bush a small, artfully made pitcher half the size of a jam pot. She filled it with milk from a few squeezes of the cow's udder and put it back under the bush. She did this every day, even during the scorching Russian summer heat, or biting cold, or snow, or fog and rain. And each morning following, the pitcher stood in its place again—empty and scrupulously clean.

One evening while closing the small shutters outside her shack Tatjana fell and broke her ankle. She dragged herself inside but could do nothing more. The next day she managed to milk her cow, but by evening the beast was bellowing hungrily though Tatjana had given her all the bread in the house.

The next day an ambulance stopped in front of the shack (one of Tatjana's customers had alerted the health service). A grumpy doctor examined her ankle hastily and, with the help of an attendant, rushed her off to the hospital. She pleaded with them to do something for her cow, but they shrugged their shoulders and drove on. None of her neighbors dared do anything for fear of the police.

In the hospital, Tatjana wept for her cow. Everyone she asked for help either shook their head or shrugged

Gnome milking

their shoulders. Her ankle was put in a plaster cast, and she was told that she would have to stay in the hospital for eight weeks because it was a complicated break. Tatjana worried herself sick over the cow, but soon news from home reached her.

As soon as the sun had set on the second day after Tatjana's accident, the shack door opened, the cow walked out and, without a tether, followed a gnome, who took her to the best grazing areas along the road. Just before sunrise she returned.

In the meantime, all the empty milk cans belonging to Tatjana's customers had been collected—along with the money that was left in advance to pay for the next morning's milk. In the shack, the cow was milked by the two strongest gnomes, and the filled cans were back at their respective addresses as the sun began to rise.

When Tatjana arrived home eight weeks later, with her ankle in a smaller plaster cast, she wept again, but this time from happiness and gratitude. There the cow stood,

the picture of health, and beside the ancient samovar on the wooden table lay the milk money for eight weeks and two days, neatly stacked.

When she went to bed that night, thinking about how she would be able to shuffle along the road the next day, she worried aloud that she would not be able to go very far.

"No need to," a voice behind her said. And when she turned around she saw five gnomes standing behind her humble bed.

"We've come to get the cow," the eldest said, critically looking at her plastered foot. "There is no question of your walking long distances for the time being. You go to sleep now and we'll take care of the rest. We hope you don't mind if we fill our own pitcher?"

Immediately the others ran off to gather the empty cans, and the eldest gnome, clearing his throat, took the cow on her way.

Legends of the Gnomes

5

Everyone knows that a brush fire during a long period of drought can be disastrous for man, animals, gnomes, and the countryside. What everyone is unaware of, however, is that many such fires occur that do not result in devastation.

Gamekeepers and foresters continually find places where small fires have briefly raged and in some mysterious way have been extinguished—sometimes very close to a dangerously inflammable area of brush or dry forest floor.

Just how the gnomes put out these fires is not known for certain. Sometimes, perhaps, by lighting a small counterfire (prairie Indian method); sometimes by speedily drilling into an underground stream and pumping up the water. But about other methods used we remain completely ignorant.

Legends of the Gnomes

6

The old writer sensed that his death was approaching. He lived in Norway, in a low cabin with book-lined walls in the neighborhood of Lillehammer, beside a mountain slope.

Next to the window, overlooking the valley, was a large table bearing paper, magazines, volumes of verse, inkpots, pens, candles, and more books, carelessly stacked.

One evening, just at sunset, the writer left his bed and went to sit at the table. He looked out over the peaceful valley with its lake in the distance, and recalled how he had lived here quietly for many years, and thought of how many books he had written and that soon it would all be over. Suddenly, a gnome jumped onto the table, seated himself opposite the writer, and crossed his legs. The writer greeted him happily.

"Tell me another story," he asked the aged gnome, who was holding his silver watch against his ear. "I can't think of any more, I've become too old."

"I don't know any more," the gnome said. "You've already written all the stories about this country. You've become rich from them."

"Just tell me one more. My hands are so tired, I can hardly write anymore," sighed the writer. (Nevertheless he placed pencil and notebook within reach.)

"All right then," the gnome said. He changed his position and stared outside. "Do you see that big weeping willow in the distance at the edge of the lake? The ends of

its branches always hang in the water. I'll tell you why.

"Long ago, one dark night, mountain trolls switched their infant daughter with the daughter of a rich farmer, kidnapping her when everyone was asleep. Next day, the poor parents couldn't understand why their daughter's skin had suddenly become so dark or why her eyes looked like black currants. But deep in the forest the trolls exulted over the blue eyes, blond hair, and soft skin of the stolen child—and they performed a joyful, thumping dance in a circle.

"The troll child grew up to be a dark, wild tomboy and did only naughty and ugly things; she loved no one and no one loved her. One day she disappeared and was never seen again.

"But in the forest, the farmer's daughter became sweeter and lovelier every year despite all the crude and rough things she saw about her. When she was seventeen she was discovered by Olav, a strong farm laborer. (Olav slept below me in the stable of a farmhouse in the valley.) He was bringing in a few lost cows from the high mountain meadow for the winter when he saw the farmer's daughter. She was sweeping the ground in front of the troll cave under the watchful eyes of the old troll mother. It was dusk, but Olav thought he had never seen anything so fair and beautiful. He immediately fell in love. As he attempted to approach, the troll mother pulled the girl inside and locked the door.

"Back in the stable, Olav asked if I would help him,

and we set off that same night. Reaching the troll hill, we saw a stream flowing from it. (Water flows through the middle of every troll hill; they use it for drinking.) Using a divining rod, I found the spring on the other side of the hill from which the water flowed. We dug a hole, and when we reached water, Olav put me into a wooden shoe and I floated into the stuffy troll cave.

"I hid myself and the wooden shoe in a dark corner of the cave and waited until the trolls left to perform their nightly crimes in the forest. Before leaving they shut the girl in a side alcove and finally locked the main door behind them. Only the girl and I remained in the somber, stinking lair. As soon as it was safe, I released the girl and said to her: 'You're not a troll girl! Outside there's someone who will suit you much better than a troll.'

"She looked quite astonished and hesitated, but finally came along with me. Outside she saw the blond giant of a man Olav; at once she fell in love with him, as he had with her.

"The three of us ran for home. But we were still deep in the forest, and before we could make our getaway the trolls learned that we had stolen their prize. They caught up with us, beat Olav until he was black and blue, and took the girl back. I couldn't do a thing.

"A week later, we tried again. This time Olav took along a horse that he had borrowed from the farmer he worked for. For the second time, I drifted along on the underground stream into the trolls' domain. But this time

the trolls had left their old mother to stand guard. When the old mother troll turned away from a bowl of porridge she was making, I quickly tossed a good dash of sleeping potion into it. Ten minutes later she was snoring away. (I had signaled the girl not to eat the porridge.)

"Again the three of us raced through the forest for home. It was much quicker this time, on a horse. But in spite of it, the trolls caught up with us, just as we were almost out of the forest. Again they beat Olav until he was half dead, then took the girl back with them—and the horse, too, of course. There was nothing we could do; no matter how strong Olav was, the trolls were stronger.

"Three weeks later it snowed. This time I managed to get two reindeer to help us. In the trolls' cave I had to wait half the night, because not only was the troll mother on the lookout but the troll father as well! Eventually I was able to sneak enough sleeping potion into their porridge to put them fast asleep.

"The reindeer transported us quickly on a small sleigh along little-known paths in the direction of the lake. The trolls pursued us, but in the snowstorm we were lucky enough to reach the edge of the lake. I knew where an old fishing boat was moored and we got to it quickly. We cut the sleigh loose, thanked the reindeer, and sent them back to their herd. The lake was still not entirely frozen. Olav and the girl climbed aboard the boat and began rowing; I skied homeward along the bank of the lake. Nothing could happen to me. Trolls have no power over us once they

leave their cave. It was almost sunrise. The last snowflakes fell; the sky opened up and, in the east, took on a yellow and red hue.

"When the boat was already a good distance across the lake, the trolls finally reached the dock. They ranted and raved, but Olav rowed with big strokes toward the other side, and the trolls couldn't reach them. The trolls didn't have much time left: when the sun shines on them, they turn to stone. Suddenly, the strongest troll seized a gigantic boulder and hurled it at the fleeing pair. The boulder did not hit the boat, but it fell so close to it that the boat capsized. The suction dragged the girl down to the depths of the lake and she drowned. For hours, Olav dived in search of her, but he had no luck. Deeply depressed, he finally swam to the bank of the lake.

"After this, Olav was inconsolable. Every day he went to the edge of the lake and stood in one spot, staring at the water. He never looked at another girl. And when he

became so old that he couldn't work any more, he continued to return daily to the same spot. In the end, he stood there the whole day long. Branches grew out of his head and roots from his feet. And then he stood there forever. He is that weeping willow you see there at the lake's edge. Even now its branches feel about in the water in an attempt to find the drowned girl.''

The gnome looked around. The old writer had grown still. His snow-white head lay upon the notebook on the table. He was dead. The gnome smiled and went over to him. He closed the writer's eyes and read what was on the paper. The last words were, ''And then he stood there forever.''

And the gnome pulled the notebook out from under the dead writer's head, carefully loosened the pencil from his stiff fingers, and wrote the remaining sentences of the story.

Legends of the Gnomes

7

Northwest of Vastervik in Sweden, where the road divides and the great elk forest begins, stands a dilapidated church. There are a few overgrown gravestones in the small cemetery beside the church. After scraping away the moss on one of these gravestones, we can read the following text:

Here lies
SIGURD LARSSON
Born the 24th of the Hay Month 1497
Died the 30th of Summer Month 1550

Only the gnomes know that the grave under this stone contains no body.

Sigurd Larsson was a rich farmer who owned an enormous estate and grew richer year by year. He was a heavily built, unpleasant man with a cruel disposition, a coarse face, and a loud voice, which he used to shout down everything and everyone. He ruled his farm laborers ruthlessly and punished them for even the slightest offense by whipping them; milkmaids were either shut outside for the night or made to sleep in the hayloft. It was a wonder that he had any staff at all; but if anyone did leave, the influential Larsson made certain they would never find work elsewhere.

Everyone on the huge farm went silently about his work and attempted to keep out of the master's way, for he had a habit of creating false crimes just so he could punish someone. For example, he once hid some pieces of gold and then pretended to catch the so-called thief when they turned up. He often swept dirt under the carpets so that he could scold the cleaning girls. A favorite pastime of Larsson's was to hide in the summerhouse at the center of the large estate and spy on his farmhands as they worked the land. He punished them later if in his opinion they had not worked hard enough.

But his greatest satisfaction was in counting and reading IOU's. He had a cupboard full of them—all from small farmers, poor families, and neighboring villagers. It was his habit to write letters each evening in which he summoned the poor wretches to the farm to press them for payment or to plague them into signing new IOU's with an even higher interest rate.

And so life dragged by on the estate: from the outside, a gay and attractive collection of buildings on a great sweeping plain; on the inside, misery, resentment, and bitter grief. In the stables, at work, and in their sleeping places, the people mumbled curses and complaints—but only into trustworthy ears, because there were also spies about. One of those trusted was the farm gnome.

Night after night, he patiently listened to the complaints of first this one then the other, giving advice when he could. From time to time he would go to Sigurd Larsson in the evening and try to plead someone's case,

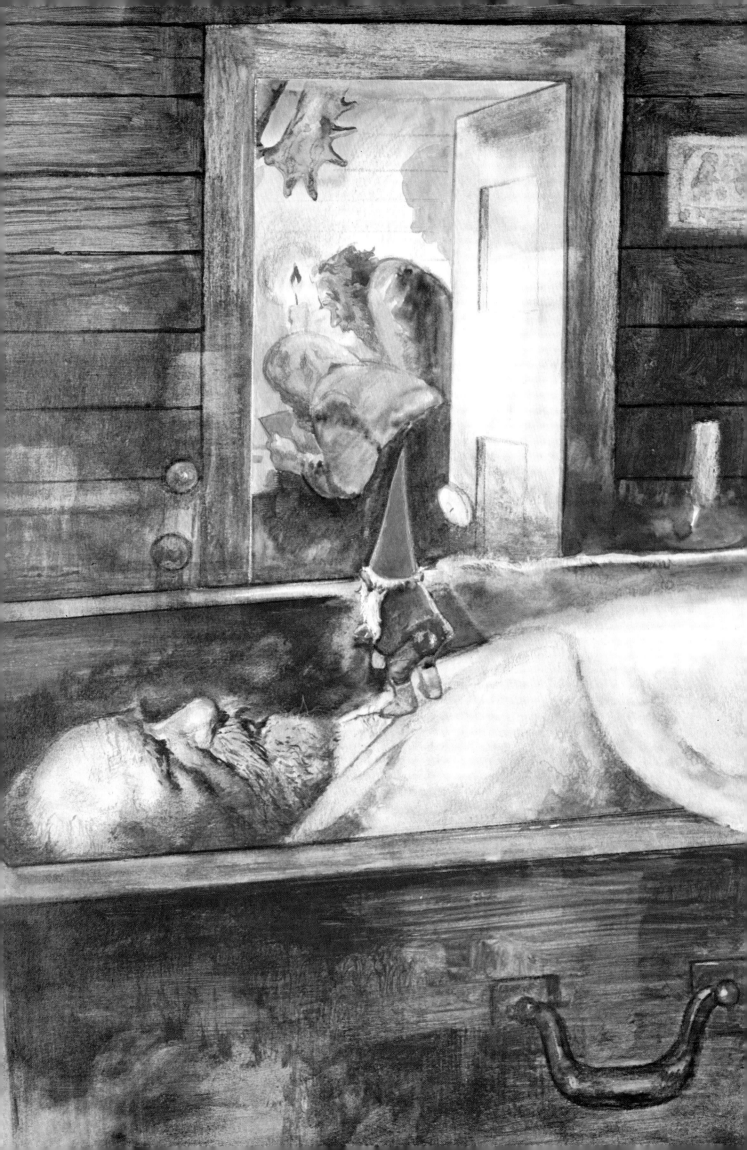

but the cruel farmer just laughed—that is, if he didn't throw an inkwell or a cup of coffee at him.

The gnome always carried himself in a very dignified way and would only say: "Just you wait, Sigurd, there'll come a time when you'll beg me for mercy on bended knee." Then the farmer would become furious and try to grab the gnome, but the gnome would always see to it that he sat in a position from which he could, with the simplest movement, escape through a chink in the wall.

Years went by. And then something began to change slowly in the big, strong body of Larsson. There were times when he felt tired, and pains shot through his arms and legs—something he'd never experienced before. At first he would just curse it away and do some cruel deed to show that he was still the same old Larsson. But his condition worsened within a few months and he began to lose weight. First a physician was sent for, then a surgeon, and then an herb doctor. None of them could diagnose his case, for all their learning, and Larsson was relieved only of a good deal of money.

After eight months, his eyes were hollow, his stomach caved in, his arms and legs were as thin as birch branches—he couldn't walk more than ten minutes without becoming tired. Finally, he went to Stockholm and Uppsala, but the professors there shook their heads, saying that there was nothing science could do to cure him.

The gnome did not let himself be seen by Sigurd for a month after his return. One evening he silently appeared when the farmer, weak and disheartened but still vicious, was going over his IOU's.

"Sigurd," the gnome said. "You're going to die."

"The farmer raised his head with a quick jerk and stared at the little man. He briefly considered throwing a book and killing the gnome, for he sat unconcerned on the edge of the table, but instead Larsson said:

"What do you know about it?"

"Everything," answered the gnome. "I even know what you need and the herb that can cure you."

And with that, he disappeared.

A week later he returned and said:

"A devil is gnawing at your nervous system and causing your muscles to dry up. They're eager to have you in hell so they can roast your black soul."

"Wait," cried the farmer, but the gnome had already disappeared. A week later he came back and said:

"I have a magic potion that can rout the devil out, but you're not going to get it." And disappeared again.

When the gnome came back during the third week, Sigurd fell on his knees and begged:

"Help me! I'll give you anything you want."

He was now just skin and bones and could hardly walk from one chair to another. But the gnome just shook his head and said:

"It will be a blessing when the world is rid of you. But first you must suffer some more."

A short time later, the insidious illness slowed the

working of Larsson's heart almost to a standstill.

And then came the morning when he did not awaken. It was the barber who found him and pronounced him dead. The priest prayed over his body, for the rest and peace of his departed soul. Everyone breathed a sigh of relief.

But the farmer wasn't dead. It only seemed that way. His heartbeat was so slow and breathing so slight that they escaped the barber's attention. But the farmer had heard everything and could just barely see through his almost closed eyelids. For the rest, he was totally paralyzed.

For a day and a half he lay in state in the death room. Servants and maids paid their respects by hissing curses at him and making faces.

On the evening before the funeral, the gnome

appeared by the coffin and said to Larsson:

"Do you hear that noise in the room next door? That is your wife and the overseer, who have broken open the cupboard. They're tearing up the IOU's."

The next day Larsson saw the light disappear as the lid was screwed onto the coffin. Then, with a deadly fear in his heart, he felt the movement of the hearse. He wanted to scream and knock on the coffin lid but he could do nothing: he was completely paralyzed. Still later, he heard dull thuds as shovelfuls of earth fell onto the coffin. And the sound of the priest's voice and the mumbling of the bystanders became more and more faint. Larsson had never known such fear. When the gravedigger finished filling in the grave, the people went home, saying, "He was nothing but a scoundrel. What luck to be rid of him."

Late that first night, eight gnomes gathered around the grave. They dug away the earth above the coffin with their shovels and pried opened the lid. The farm gnome poured a few drops from a bottle between the livid lips of the farmer. Larsson suddenly felt a wondrous power flowing through his body and opened his eyes.

"This is the healing potion," the farm gnome said. "But before we make you well you must promise never to return here. Blink three times if you agree to this."

Sigurd did so. The gnome poured a few more drops between his lips.

"You will become a woodcutter in a forest far away. Promise."

Sigurd obeyed. His heart began to beat faster and his blood began circulating. He could even lift his hand.

"You will need to use this potion for the rest of your life," the gnome said. "We will ask our brothers in the forest to provide you with it every three weeks. Don't come sneaking back here, for then you will die properly."

He then emptied the whole bottle into the farmer's mouth. Sigurd sat up shakily and then stood upright in the coffin. He could hardly believe that he was alive again. Climbing out of the grave, he breathed the cool night air. Later he could not recall if it was the fumes from the bottle or his own weakened state—but he came to his senses to find himself sitting beside a wood fire in a dark forest far from his former home. Gradually his strength returned and he lived on for another twenty years—in great poverty but happy to be alive.

Three days after Larsson's funeral an inscribed tombstone was placed above his grave. (The gnomes had filled it in again very carefully.)

At the farm there were no more beatings or nagging—on the contrary, everyone went about his work with pleasure, feeling better than ever. Larsson's wife proved to be a good mistress in whom people could place their trust. There was laughing once again on the estate, and the girls sang and danced freely at holiday time.

The summerhouse was no longer used for spying on people, but for gay Saturday night parties and long Sundays with plenty to eat and drink.

Legends of the Gnomes

8

Northern Siberia is covered by a sparse forest, half the size of Europe, called the taiga. There are also mountain chains, discovered only in 1926, in which perfectly preserved frozen mammoths have been found.

In the winter there are three hours of daylight and temperatures hover at 55 degrees below zero; amidst these bleak conditions, the northern lights offer a show of dumbfounding beauty.

Fur-bearing animals inhabit the area—the fox, small gray squirrel, lynx, mink, marten, wolf, bear, also reindeer and shaggy-haired wild ponies. Large-limbed, hardy gnomes with piercing eyes also live in the taiga; unlike woodland gnomes, they are not invariably friendly and can be vicious if crossed. These gnomes often tease the trappers who, owing to the nature of their work, spend long weeks tracking through the icy taiga. The gnomes spoil animal tracks, cause avalanches, remove trailblazing marks, imitate wild-animal calls in the night, and warn animals of the hunters' approach.

North of Oimyakon there lived a gnome named Kostja, who was much more mischievous than the rest. He was a giant of a fellow, more than half again as large as woodland gnomes—even measured in his socks. He made everyone in his part of the forest tremble with fright.

If he discovered hunters in his territory, he went to them and demanded they pay a toll: the best pelts they had. If they hesitated, he threatened to make their reindeer ill or cause them to fall off a cliff, knowing full well that the hunter depends on the reindeer for his livelihood.

Eventually all this came to the attention of the gnome king of Siberia. A stream of complaints had reached the court. Gnomes were getting a bad name, and the king decided that it was time to teach the scoundrel a lesson. So he summoned a pair of wise old gnomes; they conferred for a day and a night, and hatched a plan. Then the younger and more clever of the two was sent off to do the job.

First, the clever gnome went to the wild ponies and spoke to the leading stallion. An hour later a dozen swift ponies swarmed toward the south and formed a giant half circle. They would act as a lookout: as soon as one of them saw a hunter entering the territory of the malicious gnome he was to alert the stallion. Meanwhile the gnome galloped off to the roosting place of a friendly owl. He returned to the half circle of ponies, the owl flying alongside.

After a two-day wait the ponies signaled that a hunter, riding a reindeer, was heading in a northerly direction. The ponies were thanked and sent home, and the stallion, the owl, and the gnome followed the hunter's tracks in the snow. They waited until he had set his tent up for the night, then the gnome appeared and spoke to him. The man said he would be happy to cooperate with them in punishing the wicked gnome, as he had heard many unpleasant stories about him. Leaving the hunter with his instructions, the stallion returned the gnome to the court.

Next evening, as the hunter once more set his tent up for the night, Kostja appeared and demanded a pelt.

"Good, good," said the hunter. "Here, take my very best, a mink of excellent quality."

The gnome growled suspiciously but took the fur and disappeared with it into the forest.

Two days later, at twilight, he accidently passed the same place again and was very much surprised to see a most beautiful fox pelt hanging on a branch just over the spot where the tent had stood. The gnome remained at a distance and continued to stare silently at the pelt for a full

half hour. He then circled around it three times, peering at it suspiciously; finally, he decided that it was all right. The hunter must have forgotten it. A windfall.

In his greed, Kostja did not see the owl, pressed tightly against the trunk of a spruce tree a short distance away, and he began to climb the tree to retrieve the fox pelt. It had a smooth trunk with few branches, and the gnome had to use his hands and feet in order to get a firm grip. When the gnome was halfway up, the owl suddenly swooped down and snatched the cap from his head. The gnome ranted and raved so much that he lost his grip and fell to the ground with a thud. Too late: the owl, with the cap in his claws, was flying high above the trees toward the palace.

The icy night was far from agreeable to the bareheaded gnome. The only thing he could do was to pull the collar of his jacket over his freezing head and hurry home. He was so angry that he stayed indoors for a week (giving his poor wife a terrible time). Now, he could have made a new cap by making felt from some of the furs in the house, but a cap is an irreplaceable possession for a gnome; he wanted his own back, no matter what the consequences.

Although he was wicked, this gnome was far from stupid. He knew that there was more to the matter than met the eye. Even so, it was ten days before he could summon up the courage to cover his head with two of his

wife's kerchiefs and present himself to the king. He had lost weight and felt humiliated.

At court he was coolly received and had to wait three hours before the king and his council granted him an audience. The king sat on a dais. He was smaller than the gnome but he radiated an air of absolute authority. There, at the king's feet, lay the cap.

"I hope that this has taught you a lesson, Kostja," he said. "None of us are angels, but your behavior has left much to be desired. You may have your cap back if you give away all your furs to the first hunter you see. Do you understand?"

"Yes," mumbled the guilty gnome.

The king placed a foot under the cap and flipped it into his arms, saying: "Put it on outside. You may go."

The giant gnome felt very small. He turned around, went out the door, left the palace, and did what he had promised, for gnomes, be they good or bad, always keep their word.

It was the end of January. A severe northeasterly wind was blowing and the thermometer registered 30 degrees below zero. Everything in the fields and woods was frozen stiff, and the gnomes' outdoor activities were reduced to a minimum, unless, of course, someone was in need of help.

In the cozy, safe houses under the trees, games were played and stories told. Imp Rogerson thought up something new every night. His great-grandfather had known Wartje, the magic goldsmith who dared to do everything, and had told stories about him to his son, who had told them to his son, who told them to Imp.

One night, Imp's twin daughters, tired and sleepy-eyed from playing, sat at their father's feet and begged for a new story about Wartje.

"Have I told you how Wartje got back the gold and precious stones a dragon had stolen and returned them to the elves of Thaja?"

"Yes."

"And how, to save the life of a little human girl who lay dying, he plucked a life-giving herb from an island in Siberia that was guarded by a ferocious dinosaur?"

"Yes."

"And how, during a storm, he slipped off the back of an osprey and fell into the middle of the bewitched lake of Warnas, and was brought to shore by a blind carp?"

"Yes."

"And how he was captured by the trolls?"

"No."

"All right then. Wartje was always falling out with trolls. As he was far too clever, they couldn't stand him. You remember that Wartje had three houses—one in Poland, one in the Ardennes, and one in Norway—so that he could carry out his many tasks. In Norway he always had problems with jealous trolls. Now, Wartje rode a large fox who ran more swiftly than the wind. He could travel from one house to another, even with his wife and goldsmithing tools aboard, in less than one night.

"Once when Wartje was in Norway, the trolls dug a

hole alongside a path he normally used. Wartje and his fox
passed that way a few nights later. They had been on a
long, tiring journey and were both extremely hungry.

"As they neared the trap, the fox smelled a strong
odor of mouse and dashed into the hole. (The trolls had
crushed a number of mice with their filthy fingers and
smeared them on the sides of the hole.) Before Wartje and

his fox realized it, they were trapped. Wartje must have been very tired to have been tricked in such a fashion. But they could do nothing. The trolls took them through an underground passage into their cave and shut Wartje behind bars in a side alcove. The fox was put in chains.

" 'Now you will forge gold for us,' the trolls said to Wartje. 'We'll never set you free.'

"Every day they pushed a nugget of gold through the bars and ordered:

" 'Make a bracelet, a ring, a necklace. You won't get a mouthful of food until they are finished.'

"And they threw an old bone to the fox, that is, if he was lucky enough not to get a well-placed kick instead. Wartje had to follow their orders because he had found no way to escape, and he had to think of the plight of the poor fox as well.

"The trolls wore the bracelets, rings, and necklaces on their misshapen arms, necks, and sausage-like fingers. They danced and danced in their filthy cave until the sweat ran off their bodies and the place stank worse than usual.

"When, after two weeks, Wartje had not returned, his wife, Lisa, began to worry. Wartje had often stayed away in the past, but never as long as this. One night she went out to search for him, which was very brave of her. She asked all the animals she met if they had heard anything of her husband, but none of them had. At last, at the foot of the mountains Lisa ran into a rat who had fled

the troll cave where Wartje was held captive, because the stench was too much even for him.

" 'You'll never get him out,' the rat said, 'They'll only catch you as well. I can tell you that they keep the key to the side alcove in the third crack in the wall beside the fireplace. On the main door there is only one bolt, but it is too high for you to reach.'

"That evening, Lisa made a plan. She gathered together some pans, rotten eggs, beans, and devil's dung (asafetida), a gum resin that trolls adore but can never get because the plant which produces it grows in faraway Persia. They love it because of its horrible smell.

"Lisa disguised herself as a sorceress with a tall pointed cap covering her own cap and a black robe, set up a wood fire on a flat rock not far from the troll cave, and began to cook her brew. Before long the revolting smell was wafted into the cave and the trolls, following their noses, waddled curiously outside.

" 'What's going on here?' they asked suspiciously, a bit afraid of the little sorceress.

" 'Nothing exceptional, noble sirs,' Lisa replied. 'I am a poor sorceress and am preparing my simple evening meal.'

" 'Hummm,' growled the trolls enviously. 'It smells good.'

" 'Would you like to taste some?' Lisa asked. 'But only a mouthful for each, as this is all I have.'

"The trolls tasted a mouthful and declared that they had never tasted anything so delicious.

" 'I see you enjoy this simple food,' Lisa said. 'It happens that I will be here tomorrow. Do return, with your entire family. How many people should I count on?'

" 'Five,' the trolls said, more dim-witted than usual because they could think of nothing but the heavenly taste on their tongues.

" 'Good. Come just before sunset, then. You can let your own fire go out because I will prepare enough food to last for three days. I won't be here myself, as I have business in the neighborhood.

"The next evening the trolls found five portions of

eggs, beans, and devil's dung and a huge pan with enough in it for the next three days.

"While the trolls were stuffing themselves, the little woman climbed atop their chimney and lowered herself quickly into the cave. (The lazy trolls had actually let the fire go out.) Lisa ran to the third crack in the wall, grabbed the key, and set Wartje free. He quickly unchained the fox and, standing on the fox's back, lifted the bolt of the outside door.

"They left in a hurry. But the fox was stiff after being cooped up for so long and weak from hunger, so they couldn't maintain a fast pace. Fortunately, the trolls were so greedy that, after eating all five portions they gobbled up all the extra food as well.

"When the trolls reached home, belching loudly, they saw what had happened and cursed Wartje loudly. But their bellies were so stuffed that they couldn't move an inch; they slumped to the floor and fell asleep."

"And now to bed with you all," said Imp to his daughters.

The gnome girls were soon fast asleep in their cozy alcove bed. Mother later discovered that they had smuggled a field mouse in with them, and she put him back in his basket.

The heavy oak roots surrounding the house shook softly as the strong, icy wind blew above in the branches. But below, in the sturdy gnome dwelling, it was warm and safe—at least from trolls!

Gnome Music

Every gnome dowry chest has inside it a music box which begins to play when the chest is opened. These music boxes are highly prized and are made from wood of the best quality, with the finest spring-steel mechanisms. In most homes the music-box tune is based on the heroic poem about the legendary Swedish gnome Thym, who lived between 1300 and 1700.

the Troll Pimple ↓

the girl from Uppsala ↓

wood! ↑

the legendary gnome Thym ↓

The Song of the Troll

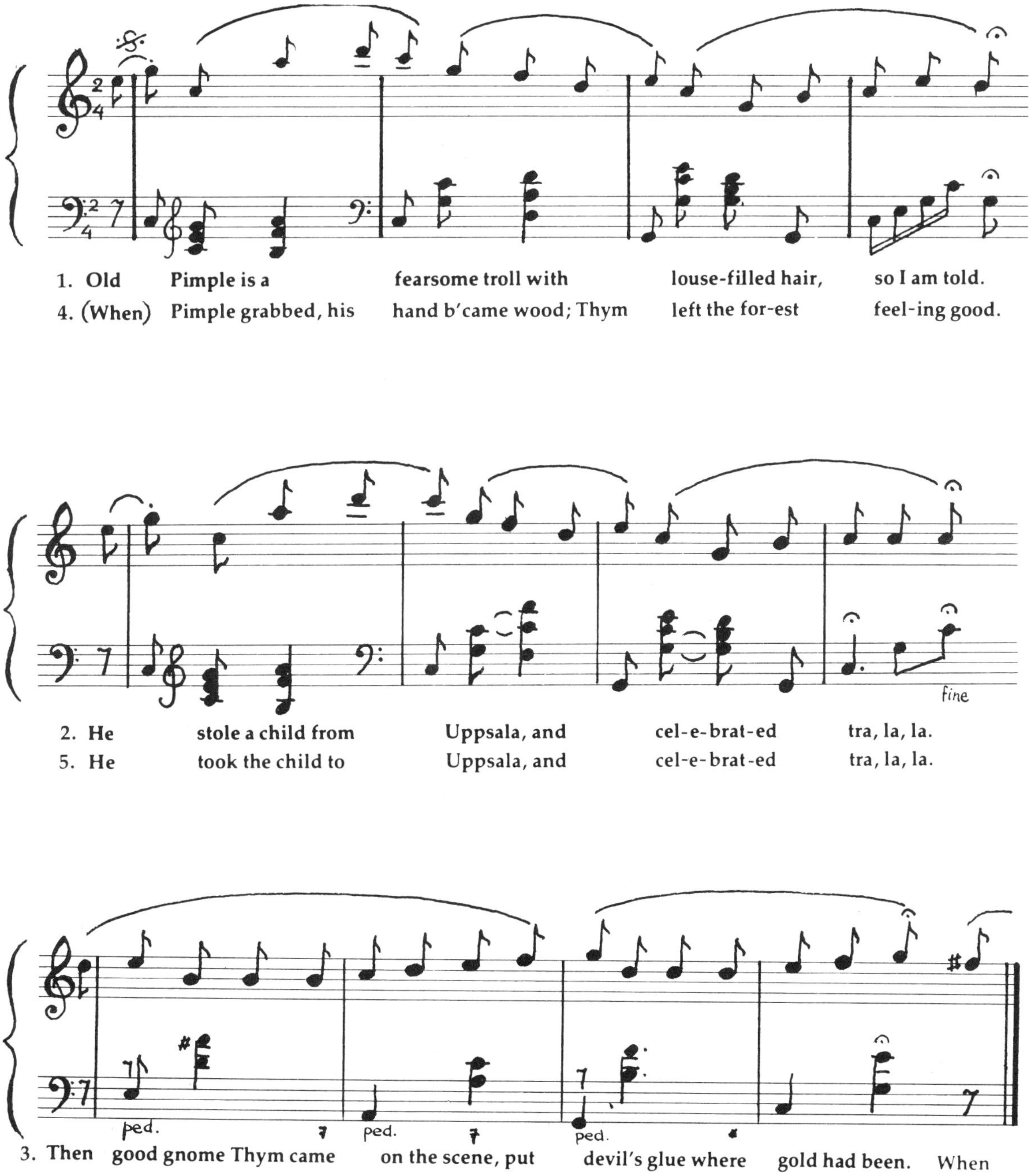

1. Old   Pimple is a   fearsome troll with   louse-filled hair,   so I am told.
4. (When) Pimple grabbed, his hand b'came wood; Thym left the for-est   feel-ing good.

2. He   stole a child from   Uppsala, and   cel-e-brat-ed   tra, la, la.
5. He   took the child to   Uppsala, and   cel-e-brat-ed   tra, la, la.

fine

3. Then   good gnome Thym came   on the scene, put   devil's glue where   gold had been.   When

ped.

2.
S.

When a gnome goes to the toilet he doesn't lock the door: a music box plays, indicating that the room is in use. The action is triggered by a secret handle upon entering the room. The words of the tune played are not sung, but are well known. In many gnome houses, the text of the song hangs beside the toilet door, and the tune is often hummed by members of the family as they wait.

While the music box plays, the gnome spends his time usefully. In this room, over the years, many artistic objects are made— such as carved portraits, toys, and attractively fashioned household utensils.

Do Not Disturb

A Conversation with Tomte Haroldson

Eventually we were working on the last chapters, the required number of pages having been filled. One of the gnomes we often talked to during our research for this book was the now 379-year-old Tomte Haroldson. He lives in the flax fields near Amersfoort, in Holland.

One cold evening at about midnight, Tomte came unexpectedly, which he had never done before. All the doors and windows were closed against the inclement weather, but this had not hindered him.

He greeted us calmly, acted friendly but distracted, as always, and seated himself on the studio table. He apparently knew that our work was almost done and had come to satisfy his curiosity, which pleased us no end. We cheerfully gave him an acorn cup of fruit wine and a cashew nut cut into three pieces. He took a sip, turned the cup around pensively in his fingers, looked about him, and asked:

"How is it coming along?"

"Beautifully," we cried. "We're almost finished."

"And exactly as you wanted it?"

"Well, it can always be improved," we said modestly (not believing it).

"Then you think it is all right as it is?"

"Of course, why not?"

"May I see how it has turned out?"

We placed a thick pile of sketches and text in front of him and let him see everything, from the beginning. He looked at page after page without saying a word, now and then stopping us when he wanted to study a sketch or a sentence more thoroughly, and thoughtfully munched on his cashew. His silence bothered us so much that we looked at each other glumly from time to time.

He was through at 1:30 A.M. He hadn't opened his mouth since the first page, except when he wanted to chew on a nut. Our uncertainty increased. A deathly silence reigned.

Tomte raised his acorn cup and we quickly refilled it. He peered into the depths of the fruit wine, sniffed at it, then pointed at the pile of pages and asked: "Is that the whole book?"

"Well, no, not all of it," we quickly replied. "We still have to add and change a few things here and there, but all

in all, we think we've covered just about everything."

He looked at us one at a time. His gaze was deep and penetrating, as if a distant land lay behind his eyes (gnomes often have this quality).

"Am I to understand that the life and deeds of my people, for the first time in history, have been completely recorded in this?"

"Well, yes . . . more or less," we said. The little man radiated an air of remarkable authority, even though he remained seated all the while (yet another quality gnomes often possess).

Tomte nodded, and downed his drink in one swallow.

"So, this is all we have to tell you," he said, staring dreamily out the window into the darkness. "I had hoped for more."

"What do you mean 'more'? What more is there?" we asked, nervously. Our high spirits had long ago left us. Tomte didn't seem too happy either.

He pressed his hands between his knees and said, without looking up at us, "It is all very charming— delightful sketches, good stories. But something has been omitted, something has not been acknowledged. And it would be too much for us gnomes to bear if this something were left out of a book like this. Just a minute, I want to show you something." He suddenly jumped down to the floor, ran away, then came back a few minutes later carrying a leather-bound book.

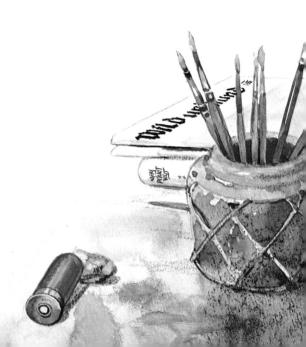

"My Family Book," he said casually. "I had it hidden outside."

He sat on the table again, put on his glasses, and turned to the middle of the book.

"We don't write down only family affairs," he said, winking his eye. "If you use that magnifying glass, you can read along. I have written it in your language."

He became serious again and indicated a date at the top of one of the pages. "I'll take just a few examples. First point: population distribution. Do you recognize this date?"

We nodded silently. It was the year we had begun our gnome studies, thinking that we were observing them without their knowing. Tomte turned to a map of one of our Dutch provinces which covered two pages. On this map, all of our camouflaged observation huts and hideaways were clearly marked and numbered.

He looked at us over the top of his glasses.

"Or were there more?"

"No."

It was a long time ago but we remembered it just as if it had been yesterday.

"Look," he said, "here it is. That year, we were spied upon three hundred and twelve times."

We were dumbfounded.

"And you thought we weren't on to you? Dear friends, you could never, with those big feet, stomp about someone's private world without being noticed. We even heard you giggling."

He turned some more pages, but it wasn't necessary. We hadn't captured them; they had captured us. It was embarrassing.

"All right," we said, defeated. "That was in the beginning. And you let us see only what you wanted us to see. But later weren't we allowed to look about freely?"

Tomte laughed a bit shyly.

"That's why I'm here tonight. Now we come to the second point: the disappointment. We were on to you and knew those aspects of our lives you were focusing on—our cleverness, our cuteness, our technical innovations, our humor. That couldn't do any harm; besides, you meant well, and that's why we went along with it. If they're so bent on portraying our outer shell, we said to one another, we'll just play along with them. Then maybe later they'll have brains enough to dig deeper."

We began to understand what he meant. Indeed, we had mainly paid attention to superficialities. He laughed again.

"But it couldn't go on that way or, rather, end that way. You both had become too dear to us for us to allow that. And that's why I'm here tonight. Sent here, I might add."

A long silence followed. It began to dawn on us that we, through our self-complacency, had only scratched the surface in our gnome studies.

"It seemed a shame to us that you might send the book to the publisher without our first having had a talk. For now we come to point three: balances. Let me begin this way. All of us come from the universe and the earth—indeed, you people say it yourselves: 'Of dust man was made, and to dust will he return!' Of course, we'll all return to the universe and the earth. But we have remained true to our origins, while you haven't. Our relation with the earth rests on harmony, yours rests on abuse—abuse of living and dead matter."

"Not everyone does this," we protested.

"Fortunately not. But mankind as a whole leaves behind it a trail of destruction and exploitation."

"Don't gnomes ever upset nature's balance?"

"No. Man runs wildly about in the world of today and lives almost always at nature's expense. The gnome has found peace in the world of yesterday and is satisfied with what it has to offer. There won't be any change in this, just as there won't be any change in salmon, who for thousands of years have swum from the middle of the ocean to the rivers of their birth . . . just as the bee who finds good pollen does a dance to call the other bees . . . or as the pigeon finds its destination thousands of kilometers away. . . ."

"That has to do with instinct. Aren't we digressing a bit?"

"Not at all. Now we come to point four: *we* have our instinct and intellect in proper balance; you have subordinated your instinct to your intellect."

"But we are only human. Our minds take over . . . that's the way we are made. Instinct doesn't offer enough security."

"It offers insufficient security only if you imprison it under a glass bell. Give me a little more wine."

"But human beings long for the restoration of nature, as she was in her old glory."

"And that's why we must proceed in three ways: the restoration of instinct, the restoration of balance in nature, and less striving for power."

"Why are you throwing that in?"

"Because all the other evils on earth stem from the craving for power. You know that just as well as I do."

"Don't you gnomes ever struggle for power?"

"No. We have tossed all power politics overboard."

"That is of course much easier to do in a gnome society, where you have no population problem."

"Overpopulation is something you must be able to overcome among yourselves; we have already done so."

"Is this all included in the perfect harmony that the gnomes have achieved?"

"Yes."

Here we had reached an impasse in our discussion. No doubt their world is harmonious and stable; one might even think it monotonous. But imagine meeting a stag with colossal antlers on a lonely path beside the woods: this is a sight that has not changed over the ages, yet everyone would want to see it again.

Tomte walked back and forth on the table, his hands clasped behind his back. "Fifth point: You must not think that we despise man's civilization—though nature has had to pay dearly for it—or that we can't appreciate its good points. But there is an immense gap between what you understand as progress and what we understand as progress. When we see the idiotic and ugly things you do, we can only shake our heads in wonder. I have collected a few examples of these."

He picked the book up once again, turned a few more pages but suddenly slammed it shut while he slipped his eyeglasses into the bag attached to his belt.

"It is too late now," he said. "I have a few things to do before sunrise."

"Tomorrow night at 10:30," Tomte said. He pointed at us cheerfully. "Look at you both, just sitting there. Surely you're not going to let yourselves become discouraged?"

He tapped on the manuscript.

"It will be a magnificent book. Or otherwise we can always do something about it. You can please me by adding a chapter; call it 'Why Gnomes Shake Their Heads.' "

And he disappeared.

Why Gnomes Shake Their Heads

Although a great gap lies between your idea of progress and ours," Tomte said the following evening, seated in a doll's armchair, the book on his knee, "we do follow yours from a distance. Take the example of Rembrandt van Rijn. My brother Olie knew him very well. Olie lived under an old lime tree near Rembrandt's house beside a canal in Amsterdam, and he spent countless evenings in a dark corner drawing alongside the master.

"Many times he shook his head in wonder at the stupidity and narrow-mindedness of the men who commissioned the paintings, the abuses Rembrandt suffered, and the awful poverty he endured at the end of his life. He saw the famous *Nightwatch* progressing stroke by stroke, a masterpiece now admired almost to distraction. Shaking his head and with pain in his heart, he saw how the painting was sawed down to make it small enough to fit through the door, when it was later moved to the Town Hall after Rembrandt's death.

"And what did you humans do with the good doctor Semmelweis in 1865? Do you suppose we didn't hear about it? What we had known for hundreds of years was finally discovered by man: that the delivery of an infant must be carried out with clean hands so that neither the child nor the mother will become infected. Semmelweis was simply hounded to death by his opponents."

Tomte pushed his glasses onto his forehead and looked at us.

"That is what I meant last night."

"Well, yes, but we also know this. Throughout history the most incredible stupidities have occurred. We too shake our heads at this."

Tomte lowered his glasses again and turned some more pages.

"The difficulty seems to be that humans simply do not recognize a great man in his lifetime, especially if he is an artist."

"That is because some artists create works for which the people are not yet prepared—except for a small devoted circle. Only after one or two generations does recognition come."

"In the meantime the artist has died, forgotten. Think about one of your most famous composers. I have it firsthand from Timme Friedel. Timme is a small, dreamy gnome who left Vienna in despair in 1791 and now lives in a rock dwelling in the countryside. Now, we gnomes may not have a Mozart among us, but we would surely have offered a man of such talents a more dignified way of leaving this world.

"The conversations between Mozart and Timme are written in a small book that your historians would give their eyeteeth to get hold of. Timme always knew how to help Mozart out of a somber mood. He had only to ask Mozart to give him a violin lesson to make the master laugh like a child. He would then spend hours giving Timme his lesson.

"So it was with tears in his eyes that the devoted Timme, defying daylight, snow, and rain—followed Mozart's poor funeral procession (which cost 11 florins and 56 kreuzer) on 6 December 1791. Everyone left the procession at the churchyard gate, owing to the bad weather. Timme was the only living soul who stayed on. Shaking his head he saw how the gravedigger literally threw the coffin into a pauper's grave and then hurried off to find shelter.''

Tomte shut the book but kept his finger between the pages.

''We just can't understand it,'' he said.

He turned to the following page.

''What you have done to plants and animals is also beyond description. That the elk, brown bear, and wolf have disappeared from these parts does have something to do with changes in climate, I will admit, but the extermination of the beaver was inexcusable. The last beaver was shot in 1827 at Zalk beside the Zuider Zee and we thus lost forever a dearly loved friend with whom we had had the most cordial relations and who had provided us voluntarily with a very special type of fat. And if you, with your traffic and poisons, murder the last remaining specimens of green frog, prudent toad, and yellow-bellied fire toad, it won't be simply a matter of a few more animal species disappearing.

''No. Profound disturbances in the natural balance of things will make years of extra work for us. This is not to mention the harm done to us personally by your poisons. I will decline to comment on the miserable state of birds of prey or their infertile eggs. You humans have become nature's enemies.

''Look here: of the 1,300 plant species, 700 are in danger; the succulent leaf is almost extinct. I won't even

mention the salmon, sturgeon, or shad—all river fish that have locally disappeared. Three-fourths of your people don't even know they ever existed. You can, of course, pretend to be lords and masters of creation, but that is no reason to carry on like beasts—though a beast would behave less callously."

"Look, we two are in complete agreement with you."

"I know, I know. Can't I grumble just a little? Do you know another sickening habit? I believe people leaving on vacation, as you call it, are responsible. They throw cats and dogs out of their cars, abandoning them in the woods. You should see the poor wretches. They grieve and starve in a miserable manner. One or two survive and become poachers, and then nobody is safe."

We shrugged and said:

"They are scoundrels, indeed, who should never be allowed to keep pets. But there is, alas, little to be done about it."

He nodded and picked up the book. He flipped through the remaining pages.

"There is much more in here about the destruction of our good and beautiful world, but let's stop now, otherwise it will become monotonous. Just this, though, because it so disturbs us: stop making war. In my lifetime alone there have not been twenty-five years without a war going on somewhere in the world.

"Well, that's that. I've had my say. Now we three are going to take a walk; I want to reward you both for your many years of toil."

Outside, the full moon had risen a hand's breadth above the horizon. The tree tops stood out starkly against the cloudless sky. The night was deathly still, except for the faint rattling of a train in the distance. It was mild, and spring hung in the air.

We entered a path heading southwest. Although we were both very familiar with the area, after about five minutes we no longer knew where we were. But Tomte led the way with a sure stride and we followed.

Had we been walking for an hour? Two hours? Twenty-four hours? We couldn't for the world remember. It appeared not to be a planned walk but a predestined wandering.

Time stood still and nature embraced and enclosed us like a warm sea. We were weightless; we were ageless; we knew everything that had been forgotten. Tomte had endowed us with gnome qualities for this night.

We met a fox. He stood still, sniffed at us inquisitively with no sign of fear. A pregnant doe allowed us to scratch her between the ears and stroke her thick winter coat. A hare proudly showed us her first litter of the year. Rabbits continued their games in our presence. We spoke to wild boars and a marten.

We were questioned by an owl. We watched two endlessly playful badgers. We heard the trees breathing, bushes whispering, the mumbling of moss; we listened to secret tales of centuries past; we melted into every living cell on earth, recognized every dimension, and our souls were in equilibrium and peace.

As the moon began to pale, we completed an

unfathomable journey through an unknown dimension.

Tomte raised his hand. We stood still as he continued on up a hill.

"This is the way nature can be if you remain true to her. I wish you all the best. *Slitzweitz.*"

He walked on alone up the hill. Our hearts were sad. Beside an old pine tree he turned, raised his hand once more—this time in farewell—shook his head softly but with a smile on his small face, and disappeared over the hill.

Everything fell away like old music that is suddenly interrupted. We were ordinary mortals once again. Dawn was breaking, the sun would soon rise. At that moment we saw where we were. In the flax fields, no more than half an hour away from home.

After the walk in the moonlight with Tomte, we remained in a state of mysterious intoxication for weeks. Our profound longing for the world of the Gnomes had become even stronger. The Gnomes kept remarkably quiet and it was difficult to find them.

But years later, it all started again.

N early five years had passed since we first ventured into the world of gnomes, although this time the journey was not of our own choosing but because of a summons from the gnomes themselves. It seems that when compiling *Gnomes*, our first book, we had been too superficial in our presentation of the facts, even though the gnomes themselves had kept an eye on the work and had even consented to its publication.

Anyway, they wanted to meet us far from home in order to observe and test us. Once again—the more we saw of them, the more we realized how advanced they are. They have their roots in an older and more perfect world than ours, and they listen to voices that we have neither heard nor shall ever hear. Their observation of nature goes discouragingly further than ours and they have retained a dimension that we cannot even begin to

fathom; all we can do is merely guess about the realm of old and secret fairy tales.

At first the gnomes attempted to enlighten us with their usual gentleness by lifting a corner of the veil that hides everything unknown to us. Then, however, the situation became more of a challenge and resulted in their requesting us to deliver an urgent message, which is relayed in this book.

On the advice of Mirko, our host in Lapland, who allowed us to see parts of the *Secret Book,* we have illustrated everything precisely, although it was not always possible to make the invisible visible with pen or brush. We hope to have bridged the gap in the knowledge of gnomes—a presumption that we trust they will smilingly take for what it is worth.

On the nineteenth of December of the Year of Our Lord 19—, we found tickets for a train journey to Kemijärvi in our mailbox, with stops at Bentheim, Bremen, Odense, Copenhagen, Stockholm, Haparanda, and Rovaniemi. In minute copperplate letters on snowy-white birch bark were the words:

Come, we have serious matters to discuss!

It could only be a message from the gnomes, and we could not ignore it. We were embarrassed to admit that we didn't know exactly where Kemijärvi was, but we soon found that it is in Finland near the Arctic Circle. The tickets were made out for the North-West Express leaving Utrecht on 20 December at 8:44 P.M. Lapland in winter? The thought was unsettling. What should we expect from the gnomes? We were none the wiser after a brief visit to the nearest gnome family in Soestduinen, Holland, who smiled amiably and nodded knowingly but gave nothing away.

On the evening of December 20 the North-West Express rumbled into the station at Utrecht on its way from Hoek of Holland to Sweden, and two minutes later we

were heading into the winter night for a two-day journey. We had drawing and writing materials as well as our warmest clothing with us, but we wondered whether they would be of any use at the Arctic Circle. In our ignorance we even imagined we could buy anything extra we needed there! How different it turned out to be.

Nocturnal Holland slid past us. We stared with heavy hearts as we left behind the snowy fields and woods of our beloved Veluwe in our safe homeland. After Bentheim we silently climbed into our bunks. Only after the ferry-crossing to Korsør in Denmark did it begin to get light outside and at 9:09 A.M. we entered the misty city of Copenhagen. We had ten minutes to catch the connection; soon afterward the train crossed to Hal-

singborg, Sweden. The weather was slightly better as we traveled the whole day through southern Sweden, the country over which Niels Holgersson had flown on the white goose Maarten—a thought that was unexpectedly comforting. We reached Stockholm at 5:44 P.M. Here we had to occupy ourselves until 9:10, when the night train to Haparanda departed. We had a bite to eat, and wandered around the town, visiting the town hall, the markets, and the Church of Saint Clara.

Traveling all night along the coast of the Baltic Sea, which is frozen for six months of the year, we noticed that the daylight hours were clearly shortening; only once did we see moose. We realized that there would be no more than three hours of daylight in Kemijärvi be-cause of its proximity to the North Pole. We arrived at Haparanda at 5:40 the next afternoon. The train to Tornio took us from Sweden into Finland, where we then caught the train that would finally get us to Kemijärvi at 7:27. We passed tundras and went through vast forests of Christmas trees shrouded in darkness.

In our compartment, we stared listlessly out at the deep snow. The moon broke through from time to time and once in a while we saw a house or a cluster of buildings in a snowy field hedged by interlaced branches. There were a few passengers, and they were either reading or sleeping. In a corner sat a Lapp woman in colorful dress, holding on her knee a little girl who was drawing figures on the window with her index finger.

After leaving Haparanda the wind had increased to a storm. Somewhere between Rovaniemi and Kemijärvi the train came to a jolting, screeching halt and we were given to understand that an overhead wire had fallen. Although the repair team was on its way, passengers could expect a couple of hours of delay. It was almost half past seven. Fortunately, we still had some rolls left. It was bitterly cold outside—the wind howled and the windows were misted over.

After some time the conductor, a small wizened chap with a wrinkled, yellowish face and jet-black hair, came into our compartment. Earlier we had noticed him deliberately taking stock of us. His dark, slanting eyes somehow reflected the boundlessness of this land. He motioned us into the corridor outside the compartment where no one could hear us.

"Excuse me, gentlemen," he said in broken English. "I am a Lapp. I have traveled the world, but I have retained the ability to pick up messages from afar, like most of my people. I know who you are. You were to receive instructions upon arrival in Kemijärvi to walk back along the railroad track to a small church and wait there. Now that we are delayed anyway, you might just as well get out and walk up to the church from here. If you stay between the rails the snow will be less of a hindrance. I shall help you out of the train without being seen."

So that was the plan we were to follow! It helped to relieve our uneasiness about the immediate future. In the dark, we followed him to the front of the train where he helped us with our luggage. We thanked him, allowed our tips to be returned to us, and started off into the darkness. The safe, cosy, well-lit train got smaller and smaller behind us. There we were in the midst of gigantic rustling forests, stepping over the sleepers of the railway line in northern Finland, making for an unknown point, and not having any idea of what we were doing there!

Shortly afterward we saw the train with the repair-men approaching, and as we preferred not to be seen, we hid behind some bushes in the deep snow. They passed us by and thus unobserved we resumed our journey. A few miles farther we could see a small church some way from the track. We trudged toward it. Every-thing was peaceful. It was beastly cold, but the storm had died down as quickly as it had come up. The snow was at least three feet deep. The starry sky stretched above us and there was an ominous silence.

We waited ten minutes but nothing happened. Were we too early? After waiting another quarter of an hour we walked around the church and vicarage. There were no lights in the back or the front. A feeling of panic began to take hold of us. What had we let ourselves in for? Was this some sinister joke taken seriously by two gullible fools?

Then, suddenly, in spite of the darkness, we caught sight of an old gray-bearded Lapp, standing stock-still next to a road sign. With his thumb he was pointing over his shoulder toward the forest. At last, here were fresh instructions! New courage seemed to course through our veins and we strode past him in the direction he had indicated.

Our search was brief, however, for between the trees, at the edge of the forest, was a sleigh drawn by two reindeer. We were mystified: there was no driver! Once more we passed into the secret world of the gnomes. The reindeer snorted and pawed with their broad hooves. We got in and, snuggling under a voluminous sheepskin, sped off.

We traveled for hours. The cold did not worry us and the reindeer were indefatigable in spite of the deep snow. It was dark but because of the stars and snow everything was vaguely visible. One moment we were speeding through low birch and spruce woods, then gliding over tundralike plains with withered willows, dwarf birches, and brambles. We crossed many frozen rivers. The reindeer seemed to be following a definite course and never hesitated, although we saw nothing to mark the way. Only once did they let the sleigh come to a standstill; they stood motionless with their noses to the wind. The following moment they turned in unison sharp left and were off at a gallop, only to bear gently right in a mile-wide swoop and return to their original course. A little farther on we saw the reason for this: a fat troll was lumbering over the plain. As we passed him at a safe distance, he stood still and followed our progress. The reindeer continued to gallop for a few minutes and then fell back into a trot. We got an awful shock when an enormous branch, heavily laden with snow, came down just behind us with an earsplitting crash.

Reindeer have broad hooves that enable them to walk on snow and marshy ground. Their name comes from the old Norwegian hreindýri, and the Latin name is Rangifer tarandus. They are to be found in the whole tundra- and northern-forest zones of Europe, Asia, and North America, as well as in Spitsbergen (north of Norway), Greenland, and Nova-Zembla (Russia). In North America they are called caribou and are more heavily built. Males and females carry big, irregularly branched antlers that are shed in January, after which new ones grow. They reach almost seven feet in length and almost five feet in height. Color: brown in summer, grayish white in winter. They are excellent swimmers and tireless trotters whose hooves click when

they are on the move. The sleigh has to be some way from the animal because their droppings fall far behind them when in full gallop. They live in a wild or in a domesticated state. During the rutting season in September and October the old solitary bulls surround themselves with females. Twenty-eight to thirty-four weeks later a calf is born and becomes fully grown in a year. Reindeer are day creatures that feed on reindeer moss, grass, herbs, buds, and bark. Domesticated reindeer (especially in Siberia and Lapland) always live outdoors in herds; they are left to themselves and are followed by man when their great "trek" begins. Their greatest enemy is the wolf. In the Arctic, reindeer are of supreme importance to man. In their wild state they are mainly used for meat, and when tamed they supply many of man's basic needs: food—meat and milk (22% fat, 11% albumen, 3.5% sugar); clothing—hides, wool, needles (bone), and thread. They can be used for pulling, carrying, or riding. Below −40° F. it would be deadly for a man to breathe through his mouth—even then air exhaled through the nostrils will freeze on his upper lip. But reindeer can keep trotting for hours at a temperature of −65° F. As draft animals they are prone to whims, but a wise driver can handle them easily. He uses a long pole as a driving unit with which he only has to touch the reindeer lightly to keep them moving.

Suddenly we heard a faint sound as if a single note were being blown on a horn. The nearer we got, the louder it became. We came to a small clearing in the spruce and birch wood, where the reindeer stopped and stared to the right toward the sound. Our hearts leapt. After all the tedium, worry, and uncertainty of the journey, there was an old and trusted sight: a gnome standing on a tree trunk. He was blowing an immensely long horn, but when he saw us he stopped and walked toward the sleigh. Climbing onto it he said, "Good evening. Welcome! I was just blowing the Midwintertune,* as today is Sunturn. I am Mirko, and for the time being I will be your host. Marvelous that you came so quickly. Please get out."

In no time at all, he had unharnessed the reindeer. It was astonishing to see him untie the frozen leather straps so deftly with his tiny hands. He did not want us to help him and when we were about to take our suitcases out he said with a wink, "Leave them there. We have no thieves here."

Mirko had given the reindeer some yellow biscuits that they crunched crisply before calmly walking off and disappearing among the trees. We glanced at each other. The moment had arrived when we would be told why the gnomes wanted us, we thought. Did they want to honor us or punish us? We managed to say nothing in spite of our curiosity and followed Mirko to a small hut under the trees. It turned out to be a sauna. A glowing stove stood in the corner. "This is a deserted sauna," Mirko said, "that once belonged to forest workers. I fixed it up a bit. You must be tired. Go in it for an hour and rest. After that you must sleep." As we undressed he

* *The purpose of the Midwintertune in the twelve nights around Christmas is to keep bad spirits at bay as well as the Wolf Riders of the Wild Hunt.*

doused the hot stones on the stove with water at an
enormous rate. Thick steam resulted and the heat rose
alarmingly. We stretched out on the wooden benches
and allowed him to splash us now and then with cold
water and to beat us with birch twigs. He didn't seem to
mind the heat at all. The speed and vigor with which it
all happened is only to be found among gnomes. After
an hour he said, "Now outside into the snow! Roll
around and around, but not for too long since you aren't
used to it."

We did it and somehow managed to come out alive.
It felt fantastic. When we returned indoors the weariness
in our limbs had disappeared. Instead we felt a heavy
languor. Mirko had let most of the heat out of the hut.
Two steaming plates with wooden spoons were waiting
on one of the wooden benches. "Mushrooms in reindeer
cream," our host said. "Enjoy your meal and then try to
sleep."

He vanished through a vertical split between the
boards above the skirting. We emptied the plates. We
had never tasted anything like it. Everything that light,
air, sun, moon, and earth could produce seemed to be in
it. Then we stretched out on the benches and fell into a
deep slumber.

When we woke up it was either still dark or dark
again. The shadowy beamed ceiling of the cabin was
miles above us and the bench seemed to be an immense
wooden plain. We heard a voice: "My apologies. I should
have warned you, but I found it more amusing like this.
You must understand that it was necessary. Besides, it is
an honor accorded to very few humans: Jules Verne for
example, Hans Christian Andersen, and of course the
Grimm Brothers."

We sat up and gazed into the half-serious, half-
laughing eyes of Mirko. He stood behind us on the bench
and all of a sudden we realized that we were as small as

he was! After the initial shock, we burst out laughing. We had pointed green caps on, green smocks and trousers, and we wore felt boots. Not only were we as small as a gnome, but we had their proportions, complete with tummy, heavy torso, and big head, and *we could see in the dark just as if it were light, not to mention the fact that we smelled every detail around us as if everything had a strong aroma.*

"This is the guest attire," Mirko said. "You will feel perfectly comfortable in it." He showed us a gilt-edged, leatherbound book that he had been hiding behind his back plus our drawing and writing things, all of which were reduced in size. "Jot down everything that happens to you from now on into this," he said simply, handing us the book, which had a little golden lock. Inside we found blank sheets in loose quires.

The hut creaked as outside the wind howled through the trees. The storm had returned in full force.

From now on we will occasionally interrupt our travelogue with details of the customs, household objects, machines, and other secrets we came across in gnomeland.

NEW YEAR AT THE ARCTIC CIRCLE

"Follow me," Mirko said amiably, as he sprang off the bench. We hesitated a moment because of the enormous height, but once we dared to jump we landed lightly and painlessly. The split through which Mirko had vanished a few hours ago had appeared no bigger than a rat hole, but now we could walk through it standing upright. Beyond it was a dark passage. "This connects my house with the sauna cabin," Mirko said, taking a lantern from the wall and deftly lighting the candle with a tinder. "It is 330 feet long; we'll be there in no time. We could have gone above ground but without cross-country skis we couldn't go far in this fresh snow, and I've left them at home. Anyway, in this storm there is the danger of falling branches."

Because of the reduced gravity, we found moving just as easy as we had found jumping. Not only absolutely but also relatively we were lighter: our body content had diminished three times, our body surface twice.

Finally we were led through a door jammed between two tree roots and into another passage. We could hear from the sound of the raging storm that the passage to the right ended in the open air. Mirko opened the doors

of wall cupboards that contained all kinds of skis. "If we go out, choose a pair. They are indispensable in fresh snow. I made them all myself."

We took a passage to the left. There was no polecat trap, as we expected. A little farther on we came across a revolving door trimmed with most peculiar brushes. "Hair of the woolly rhinoceros," Mirko muttered as he turned it. "They have been extinct for the last ten thousand years. Nothing that creeps or has four legs can get through here. My house is built under a cluster of rocks because the woolly rhinos and mammoths used to destroy an awful lot. This house is thirty thousand years old. I shall let you see a map that shows the movement of the animals as far as England."

We asked him how he got hold of the hair if the animals died out so long ago.

"Wait, wait. That will soon be clear," said our host.

Finally the passage ended with a few stairs at a copper door that led into a boot room. Inside was a rather crudely painted hope chest and another door.

Mirko knocked on it significantly. "Just you wait," he said.

We were puzzled but thought it better left as it was.

"Another guest was to have come this evening," resumed Mirko. "But I think this storm is too much for even him."

We went to the table. Everything happened here with a timeless rhythm, it seemed, and the fare set before us was a dream. We held hands.* There were parasol mushrooms, chanterelles, spice cakes, mountain raspberries, bilberries, red whortleberries, sour cream and hazelnuts, and yellow Chinese tea.

"How can you get hold of all this in the winter?" we asked.

"That is what our cooling space is for," said Mirko.

Elsa scolded a lemming that was gnawing on a Christmas decoration. "The Lapps call lemmings reindeer mice," laughed Mirko. "Lemmings are all nibblers."

Every now and then the house trembled. "There is a tearing snowstorm," said Mirko, pointing upward. "If you were to go out now, you would risk being found hundreds of yards from here after the storm. Our visitor will have to seek shelter whether he wants to or not." Having said this, our host became absorbed in thought.

(travelogue continued)

Mirko slipped past us through the second door into the living room, and we followed. An ancient smell of resin filled the room, and candles flickered. Two lemmings were playing on the floor and we saw a cleverly designed rocking-chair cradle. Mirko took a pretty female gnome by the hand and said, "May I introduce Elsa?"

She could not have been more than 110 years old, as was Mirko. "How nice to see you in person!" she said.

There was a festive atmosphere, rather like home when visitors are expected for the holidays. Two adorable babies lay in the cradle, and they laughed when we tickled them. "Pretty children," we said.

"They are Milo and Annie," Elsa said tenderly. "We'll soon go to the table. Just sit quietly for a while, then we'll have tea."

As he filled his pipe Mirko remarked, "It is almost Christmas for you people. Yesterday was Sunturn, the lowest rise of the sun, thus the shortest day, although that is actually on the twenty-first of December." He regarded us mysteriously as he said, "We still have four days left!"

* *Before every meal, the gnomes hold each other's hands and silently wish each other a successful meal.*

The cuckoo clock struck 11:00 A.M., but time here did not seem to exist. We still sat cosily smoking at the table.

"One game and then to bed," said Mirko. He rose and turned back the carpet. A huge gooseboard* was drawn on the floor, but instead of geese there were dinosaurs; instead of a prison was a troll's den; instead of a well was a floating iceberg. The pawns used in the game were bronze figures of prehistoric animals and the ivory dice were from mammoth tusks. Everything was decorated with secret markings, scrolls, and flowers. The

* A gooseboard is used in a dice game for children in Holland.

chips were lumps of gold. We had played two games when Mirko announced: "And now to bed! Slitzweitz."

We were surprised to see a well-known portrait when he opened the doors of the sleeping alcove. Mirko must have found a postage stamp in one of our pockets and hung it up out of kindness.

Then the moment came to go to the bathroom. Inside, a music box played a lively trepak, a cossack dance in 2/4 time that was very amusing. The seat was beautifully painted and quite comfortable.

Elsa breast-fed her babies while we undressed, as if this was the most natural thing in the world, which of course it is.

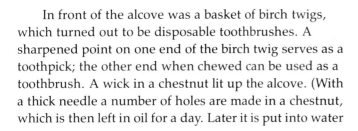

In front of the alcove was a basket of birch twigs, which turned out to be disposable toothbrushes. A sharpened point on one end of the birch twig serves as a toothpick; the other end when chewed can be used as a toothbrush. A wick in a chestnut lit up the alcove. (With a thick needle a number of holes are made in a chestnut, which is then left in oil for a day. Later it is put into water

to see which end turns upward. In that side a hole is bored that holds the wick. Finally the chestnut is placed in a bowl of water and the wick is lit. It can burn for twelve hours.)

We called "Slitzweitz" again and closed the alcove doors behind us. The air was quite fresh for being so deep in the rocks. The house still shook in the storm but here below it was warm and safe. We discussed what had happened to us and guessed how long it would be before we knew what the gnomes wanted next. On one hand it seemed as though we had lived here for years, but on the other we had a growing sense of alarm as to how we would ever regain our normal size. As it was, we just had to have faith in the gnomes. It was as it was, and we were being shown things of which no other living soul would dream. For the time being we began drawing some of our experiences to this point, and that filled up the first thirty pages in the book that Mirko gave us.

The blue print is made with indigo-drenched linen on which figures have first been drawn in wax or loam. The dye is absorbed by the linen fibers except where they are covered with wax or loam. Here they remain uncolored.

This is called negative blue print (white on blue), which is more beautiful than vice versa.

In Europe, indigo was made from the woad plant (Isatis tinctoria). The powder starts off red and becomes blue when exposed to the air, through oxidation.

A sound in the living room awakened us and we opened the alcove doors. Elsa went by in her birthday suit on her way to the bathroom. Prudery does not exist among gnomes. Natural purity is the order of the day, just as it is with animals. The cuckoo clock struck six. When Elsa was finished we took turns in the bath, which was made all the cosier by the storm outside.

At breakfast Mirko said, "Our guest is not coming for the moment. He has sent a telepathic message." He continued thoughtfully: "The question is, what must I do now? He won't be here before the New Year."

What could the mysterious guest have to do with our visit to Lapland?

Mirko said with a laugh, "Don't think that you have come here for nothing. But I have agreed to wait for him before I . . . no, I'm not going to say it yet. First we must pay a visit to the woolly rhinos!"

Gnomes hurry only when necessary. Their patience is as boundless as that of animals. Hurrying through a meal is considered foolish and an insult to the hostess. Indeed, they live so long that there is plenty of time . . . and they live so long by taking plenty of time! Moreover, they savor every morsel with their extremely well-developed sense of smell and, consequently, of taste.

We began with soup that tasted like the smell of a sunny wild-strawberry-covered mountainside. Then Mirko said, "First, a tune!"

It is not unusual for gnomes to interrupt a meal for amusement. They believe that classical music has a character-forming influence on babies from birth. An ancient lullaby was sung that we later saw in original pointed-cap writing.

On returning to the breakfast table, we found we could eat relatively more than beforehand. As a result of our diminished size, our body surface was relatively bigger in contrast to content, and the rate of digestion increased.

Ancient Cradle Song of the Gnomes

Tuuti lasta, tuuti pientä,
tuuti lasta nukkumahan.
Laulan lasta nukkumahan
uuvutan unen rekehen;
käy unonen ottamahan,
kultaisehen korjahasi
hopiasehen rekehen!

Sleep little child, Sleep little one,
Sleep little child, fall asleep quickly.
I sing my little one to sleep
lull him to sleep in the sleigh of dreams;
come, sleep, hide him softly.
Son of sleep, come carry him away secretly
in your golden cradle
in your silver sleigh!

At midnight, having spent more than four hours at the table, we left the house. Everything creaked in the wind and snowflakes tumbled in at the far end of the passage. We arrived in a long passage by way of the deserted, cold sauna.

"This passage was dug by the blind prehistoric mole,"* said Mirko. "He did not have a permanent home and was always digging around for females." Mirko increased his pace to a canter. After twenty minutes we paused to swallow a couple of caraway seeds.** New strength poured into our limbs and away we went.

After three quarters of an hour the passage sloped downward. It got colder. "Now we are in the permafrost," our host said, "the perpetually frozen earth. Watch now."

We stepped into an ice-cold, dimly lit space. Two enormous rust-colored hairy rhinos stood in front of us. A third lay in pieces on the ground. "They froze so instantaneously when they were overtaken by a snowstorm in the last ice age that the grass is still between their teeth," Mirko told us as we climbed onto their horns. "My father and grandfather hacked them free bit by bit. We use those pieces on the ground for fur and leather supply.

"The reason it is so light here is because of an ever-phosphorescent stone.*** In ancient times it was in a dragon's den in Norway. My grandfather built a couple in here."

* *Talpa caeca borealis major*
** *Fructus carum carvi*
*** *Lapis draconensis aureolucentis*

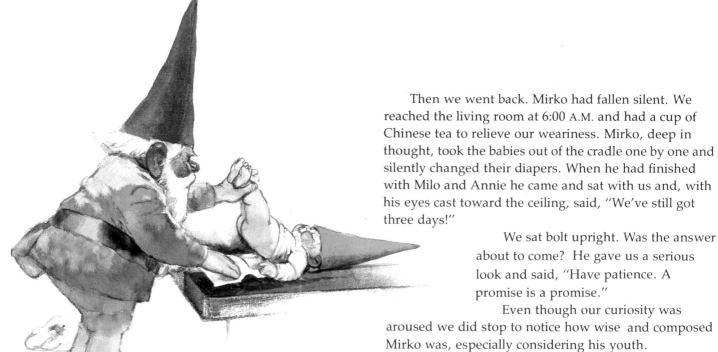

Then we went back. Mirko had fallen silent. We reached the living room at 6:00 A.M. and had a cup of Chinese tea to relieve our weariness. Mirko, deep in thought, took the babies out of the cradle one by one and silently changed their diapers. When he had finished with Milo and Annie he came and sat with us and, with his eyes cast toward the ceiling, said, "We've still got three days!"

We sat bolt upright. Was the answer about to come? He gave us a serious look and said, "Have patience. A promise is a promise."

Even though our curiosity was aroused we did stop to notice how wise and composed Mirko was, especially considering his youth.

We once again went to the table. Relaxed? Yes, that we had learned on our own, apart from the fact that we now had gnome attributes ourselves.

We then went to bed and slept from 10:00 A.M. till six that evening. The bitter Arctic wind shrieked over the plains and through the woods.

After breakfast we sat at the table for ages. It was Christmas Eve in the rest of the world. Somehow or other it was impossible to ask outright why we had been called from home in the middle of the winter. It was as if our tongues refused to do their duty. Perhaps it was because as gnomes we automatically knew what was expected of us.

When we left the table and were helping Elsa clear the dishes, Mirko stood gazing into the fire. We talked about the sea-bird disaster that had just occurred on the west coast of Sweden through the illegal spilling of oil, but Mirko's thoughts seemed to be elsewhere and he took no part in the conversation.

Suddenly he turned and strode to the boot room.

Through the half-open door we saw him open the lid of the hope chest and step inside. We were even more amazed when he began to go down and then totally disappeared.

Stairs squeaked and we could hear noises from below. Elsa too was excited and laughed shyly at us. Eventually we saw the point of our host's cap reappear above the hope chest. He had two books in his hand. One was enormous and the other was small. He stepped out of the chest, shut the lid with his elbow, and came back into the living room. There he laid the books on the table.

A green light glowed. Elsa began to blow all the candles out. When she was finished, the green radiance lay like a cloth over the table. The surrounding faces had a green glow. Mirko solemnly opened the largest book and said, "The time has come for you to peep into the Secret Book." He was silent for a moment, then went on: "These books contain everything the gnomes have recorded since the creation of the world—History, Rules of Living, Material Knowledge, etc. I wanted to wait until

our guest got here, as he has also something to say to you, but that cannot be for now. The reason you are allowed to look in this book is so that you will realize how shallow your book *Gnomes* is. Now that half the world has read that book and attached an exaggerated importance to it, things cannot be allowed to go on. It is time you grew up, and in the next few days you'll have the opportunity."

Our hearts beat faster from happiness. We had never been able to catch a glimpse of the Secret Book, which is kept in every gnome house. It appeared that the children did not even know where it was hidden in the house. Why hadn't this been able to take place somewhere in Holland? Mirko stalled our question by saying, "One of the reasons we let you come all the way to Lapland is this . . . the original Secret History Book. All other Secret Books have been taken from this one, transcribed in my house. When a gnome gets to be seventy-five years old and is registered by the local council, he comes here to do that. It takes him a couple of years. The

fact that we called you away at Christmas is due to this book having certain powers that you will soon witness, but the powers only work six days before and six days after Sunturn. That's why I couldn't wait for our guest, as you'll need a few days in which to study it."

Everyone was quiet. Elsa stared with glistening eyes and dilated pupils at the green radiance. We dared not touch the book.

"The reason I am allowed to look after such a valuable document," said Mirko, "is because we take it in turns, each for three hundred years. It might just as easily have been someone in Holland whose turn it was, but the one who looks after it has to keep it up to date." He opened the book. The letters were green and appeared to be handwritten. By chance the book was open at the chapter called "Migration of Birds." On the page a primitive globe was drawn with crosshatching, dots, crosses, secret signs, and old Norwegian runic characters. But the longer you looked the higher the map seemed to rise from the page and the bigger it got; finally it began to revolve.

The green gave way to all sorts of other colors.

"Mention something you would like to know more about," said Mirko.

"Tern!" Immediately we could witness the migration of the Arctic tern,*east and west from both Americas,

and from Tierra del Fuego to Canada and back, a journey of tens of thousands of miles that takes them to their breeding grounds at least four times in a lifespan. Even the dreaded great skuas were illustrated which steal the fish caught by the tern on their long journey and devour their eggs in the breeding places.

It was a splendid sight. The globe was now floating high above the table and revolving slowly. Also revealed were the habitats of the sooty tern, black tern, whiskered tern, white wing, common tern, little tern, gull-billed tern, sandwich tern, and the rarer sorts of these intrepid birds. If you looked carefully it was just as if the white silhouettes of the birds were flying below you.

Mirko turned to the paleontology chapter under the section "Extinct Animals." At that instant the globe disappeared. "One difference between us," said Mirko, "is that we were here long before you—you only have the fossils from which to reconstruct the past! Would you like to see a mammoth?"

A terrifying hairy giant with enormous tusks rose from the page on the spot. It kept growing until it reached the ceiling and appeared to be alive. There was no communication between the beast and us. At one point Mirko put his hand clear through the animal.

* *Sterna macrura*

Yet it was so real that we imagined we could smell it,
although it made no sounds at all.

Then Mirko showed us other prehistoric beasts. The appearance of Neanderthal man was staggering. He was busy scraping a hide with a stone; he also had no contact with us.

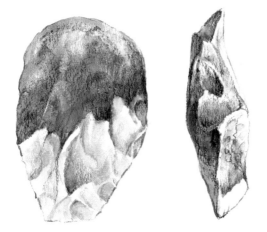

The gnomes know the whereabouts of cartloads of these stone-age tools.

We discovered that Napoleon had a gnome to keep him company on the island of Elba. Not only did they play chess together but they also took regular walks along the beach that did Napoleon no end of good, especially when he won at the contest of "who-can-spit-the-farthest."

Antonio Stradivari walked for miles through the mountains from Cremona, searching the forest for the right wood to make his incomparable violins.

The belly of a violin was made from even-grained boxwood *(Pinus silvestris)*. The ribs, back, and neck were made from Bohemian ash. The varnish he used was a special composition, the recipe of which had been lost.

He preferred trees growing above an altitude of five thousand feet because their slow growth produced closely packed rings.

He often called on the gnomes for assistance. Apart from their material knowledge the gnomes were a particular help in that inaccessible countryside.

Eventually Mirko shut the book. Time had flown

and we had by no means seen everything. It was almost dawn when Elsa began to prepare the meal.

"What is in the small book?" we asked.

"This is the abbreviated version for the children," said Mirko. "We usually read from that one before they go to bed."

After dinner Mirko took the big book to the alcove and put it against the wall at the head of a large double bed. "Look in it as much as you like," he said soberly.

We undressed quickly and, having said goodnight to them all, got into bed and began to page through the book. We saw how the boomerang and the divining rod had been developed. The chapter on healing told us whatever we wanted to know. The information rose physically from the page. It was all there—up to and in-

cluding the latest Doppler apparatus for measuring the rate of the flow in the blood vessels.

Strangely enough, the pages stopped moving every now and then while the text continued, giving us the feeling of having fallen asleep over the newspaper.

We saw the tunnels that the gnomes had dug to the magma to convert warmth into energy, which is no easy task since the layer of stone that has to be bored through to reach the glowing sill is more than 1,000 miles deep. The sill crust is 850 miles deep, according to the gnomes, who also say that the earth's core consists of a solid mass with a diameter of 2,000 miles.

We learned all about the gnomes' methods of remote sensing and semantics. There was even an illustration of Noah's Ark!

The Flood took place at the end of the Stone Age, fourteen thousand years ago. Even gnomes could not ignore the Commandment: ". . . and of all living things, of all flesh, thou shalt bring one pair into the ark to be saved with thee, man and wife they shall be." They, like Noah, could take their children as extra guests.

During the disembarkation on Mount Ararat the gnome made himself useful by directing the animals to the various continents.

Here is one of the many pictures from the Secret Book
which we would call a puzzle picture —
intended more to keep gnomelets alert
rather than just for fun!

On the other hand, there are plates that depict quite innocent shapes which, especially in the half-dark, might seem grotesquely frightening.

These teach the gnomelets to differentiate between the harmless and the really dangerous ones (same for sounds).

Stream goddesses sometimes take on the form
of irresistibly beautiful women
who calmly inhabit icy-cold waters. ——→

The man who looks at her immediately
forgets his wife and is doomed to
slavery for the rest of his life.

Gnomes are left alone
by these women.

Some have
doe eyes

or fox eyes

or hawk eyes →

Some days the stream
goddesses like to complete
their toilet on
riverside rocks;
it is remarkable
how many time-
consuming jobs the
gnomes find to do
in the area.

"Roesalkas"
are completely green
and some even have fish tails.
They are careless by nature and have no
idea of what they do to a man.
They get sick if their hair dries.

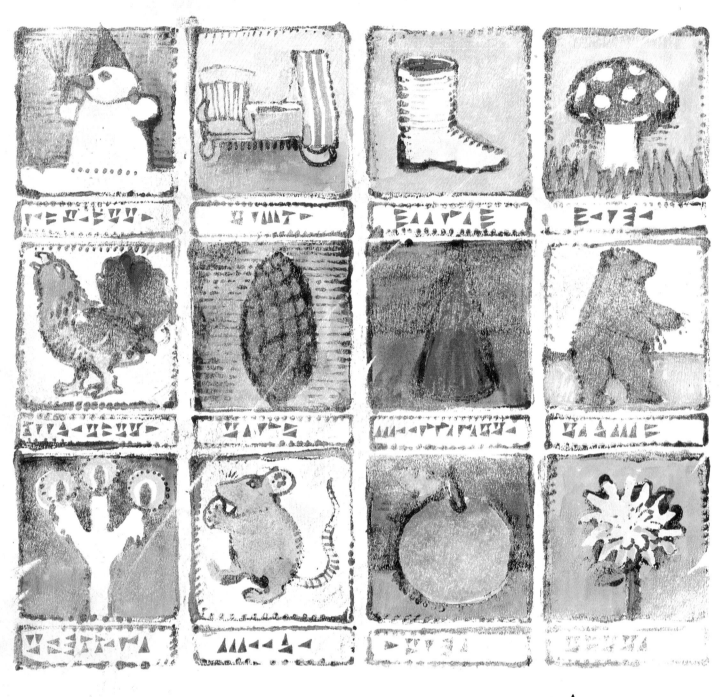

prehistoric reading board

← Pointed Cap writing from which cuneiform is derived is no longer used by gnomes.

(travelogue continued)

"May we see where the Secret Book is kept?" we asked Mirko after breakfast.

"Certainly," he answered brightly.

The lid of the hope chest lifted and we stepped inside. There was a large bright area below us that must have been situated under the living room. There were seven desks. . . .

The next morning we again took the book into the alcove. Apparently there was a lot more to it than we thought, and we had seen the previous day that this was only Part III.

One week passed.

One evening as we were finishing breakfast, the cuckoo clock struck twelve. According to our calculations it was January first.

We rubbed noses with Elsa and Mirko and wished them a happy New Year. "The storm is abating," said Mirko. "There will be no wind tomorrow but there is three feet of snow outside and it will freeze solid as soon as the wind stops. I am expecting our guest tomorrow toward evening. There are lots of trolls about and I've heard that an infamous band of ice trolls is roaming around and even tried to bring a snotgurgle to life. Our friend has to take all sorts of precautions!"

On the evening of January first we heard an urgent knocking at the copper door. Mirko answered it and who should come in . . . but a Siberian gnome! He was inches taller than us, and wore a garment of rough skins and a pointed fur cap with enormous earflaps. Below his penetrating eyes and red nose was a wild beard.

"Hello, Nicolas," said Mirko. "Welcome! You must have had a grueling journey."

The Siberian gave no reply. He turned around, unbuckled a heavy knapsack and, letting it slide off, pushed it with his foot against the wall. Then he threw his rough woolen mittens on it too. Only then did he turn to Mirko and say, stretching out a hamlike hand: "That bit of snow and wind? Don't make me laugh!"

He rubbed his nose with Elsa.

Facing us, he slowly examined us from head to toe while removing his garment, then walked off to the boot room to hang it up. When he returned Mirko said, "May I introduce you to our Dutch friends?"

The Siberian grunted and said, "Why? Aren't these the ones who knew so well that Siberians are all scoundrels and that my friend Kostja was a skin thief?"

We looked at each other. It was an awkward situation. Elsa and Mirko were embarrassed too. For the moment the arrival of the long-awaited guest was something of a disappointment. Mirko saved the day by saying, "That may be true, Nicolas Stepanowitsch, but there is such a thing as manners. Even if it were only toward Elsa and me. Now shake hands."

The Siberian sniffed, shrugged his shoulders, and begrudgingly offered us his hand. Then we sat down. Mirko went over to a cupboard and returned with a bottle and glasses. "How about a glass of mushroom gin?" he asked Nicolas. The guest gestured his assent.

We also were given brimming crystal glasses. When we had drunk to each other's health, a smile appeared on Nicolas's face. "How you always manage to make such delicious mushroom gin in Lapland is beyond me!"

He was right. It was an extraordinarily delicious drink.

In spite of our recent experience with him, we had

great respect for Nicolas. He was an enormous gnome and radiated an obstinacy that was probably well suited to his rugged existence in the never-ending taiga, a forest half the size of Europe. Perhaps this accounted for his not being the most pleasant gnome on earth.

He stretched his legs and appeared to doze off. He certainly must have had a tiring journey. No one spoke a word. Suddenly he opened his eyes, threw back his drink, and said, "A bear is trapped twenty-five miles from here. We must go immediately."

Before you knew it we were provided with saws, axes, ropes, knives, earmuffs, long underwear, and vests, which Mirko took from a cupboard in the passageway, and before long we were off on the skis. The gnomes' speed was killing. Mirko had to give us a caraway seed every quarter of an hour, otherwise we couldn't keep up.

The temperature was −30° F., but there was no wind. Forests, plains, and frozen marshes flew past. Nowhere did we sink into the snow, although it was many feet deep.

Finally, near a steep hill we saw a snow-sprinkled bear hanging motionless, jammed into a fork in a tree. He was scarcely breathing and his eyes were dull. The pressure on his ribs had probably cut off his breathing and he must have been half frozen. Mirko and Nicolas immediately began to hack at the outer side of the right branch.

When they had made a decent wedge, they climbed onto the other branch with a rope.

"You two go and stand under the bear," called Mirko. "When we let the ropes down, you must put them under the neck, foreleg, and back, and then throw the ends back up."

We climbed the tree so that we were directly below the nearly dead bear. The hairy, smelly, snow-covered body made an enormous impression on us. After three throws, the gnomes had all the rope ends and tied them to the trunk. Then they jumped down.

"Now saw on the inside of the fork," said Mirko. "Careful, because this branch will soon go crashing down."

The four of us sawed away. The tree began to crack and moved a bit. We sawed a few inches deeper. The cracking noise grew louder. The bear took one deep breath. Nicolas uttered an unintelligible bellow with lots of rolling r's.

And then, after sawing for another half an inch, the crown of the trunk gave way with an earsplitting crash and much falling snow, and disappeared into the depths of the steep slope. Now we saw how wise it had been to suspend the bear temporarily. He would otherwise have fallen fifteen feet, which would not have done any good for his frozen body. The bear would also have slid down the slope just like the fallen branch.

The gnomes climbed up again quickly, and we followed. The ropes were slowly relaxed. It succeeded! The bear must have weighed at least five hundred pounds, but we could hold him by sliding the ropes around the tree, which gave increased resistance. Apparently the ropes were as strong as iron.

At last the bear fell with a soft "plop" in the snow. When we were all down again and standing around him, Mirko took a bottle of arnica ointment out of his bag and began to rub the bear's bruised ribs with it. Meanwhile

Nicolas poured lobeline in the corners of the mouth to stimulate breathing. We rubbed snow into his limbs as hard as we could to get the blood flowing again. After half an hour the bear was visibly breathing more easily. He tried to get up but fell over each time. After a quarter of an hour he tried again. This time he remained standing, though he was swaying and completely drunk. His small eyes looked worried, but nevertheless grateful.

"How far is it to your lair?" asked Mirko.

The bear growled from somewhere deep in his throat.

"An hour! Can you make it?"

But the bear was already gone. Lumbering and sliding, he made his way from the slope until he finally disappeared into the dense wood.

"He'll make it," said Mirko reassuringly. "But he will have a couple of uncomfortable weeks. The storm must have awakened him from his hibernation."

At home the atmosphere was tense again. The trip to the bear had been a distraction from the menacing Nicolas and a welcome interruption of life under the earth, but once back again Nicolas made us feel uncomfortable.

He silently indulged in an enormous meal, interspersed with soft wine, and then stretched out in a hammock that had been slung for him across the living room and went to sleep with an ever-increasing snore.

The following night he told us that he had come to take us to Siberia and that there was no turning back. We had already apologized for our superficial handling of the first book but obviously that was not enough.

"A wonderful opportunity for your all-around improvement," said Mirko ambiguously. He must have known about this.

We tried to tell him that we thought this might be going overboard. We asked, "Who will make us big again?"

"We can do that in Siberia too," said Nicolas grimly.

"Why do we have to go to Siberia?"

"To realize why we called for you," said Mirko.

We could do no more. Besides, we felt it had nothing directly to do with our first book at all. Yet we gave it one more try: "Supposing you made us big right now so that we could go home?"

Mirko brushed aside this desperate attempt that would ordinarily have canceled out all intimacy between us and the gnomes. "I can do it," he said, "but I don't want to. You will understand everything later."

There was nothing more to do. All we could say was that we wanted to call home to report that we would be returning considerably later than we had anticipated, although of course no definite date had ever been mentioned. Mirko was more than willing and Nicolas couldn't care less.

Deep in the night we went to a village a few hours away from Mirko's house. All was quiet and still. Via an unused rat hole we got under a house and into the living room by squeezing through a crack in the floorboard. An antique telephone hung on the wall. It was ages before there was any reaction but eventually we got a crackly connection with Holland from a nocturnal voice in Helsinki.

We got our wives on the line; they were sleepy but pleased to hear from us, but less pleased when they heard we intended to stay longer. But we explained,

while constantly juggling the telephone from ear to mouth, that we simply could not help it.

When we hung up, both rather moved, Mirko said, "You might not be looking forward to it, but it will be a marvelous experience, just you wait!"

At the time we did not agree with him whatsoever, but Mirko brushed aside all our objections, fished a lump of gold out of the depths of his pocket, and, laying it beside the telephone, said: "That ought to be enough."

Then we returned. No one spoke.

Two nights later we were to depart, but first Mirko

wanted to talk to us alone. Our thrill at the revelations in the Secret Book was tempered by the recent occurrences, partly because we had not managed to see the complete Book. We asked once but he silently shook his head. "That last part is what it's all about," said Mirko. "You are not ready yet to see the core. One or two things still have to happen to you."

He became very serious. "Don't think we behave without reason. This is what I mean: In the first place I'm not allowed to show you the complete Secret Book. Something has to happen first. Second, there wouldn't

be enough time. While transcribing the Secret Book, which consists of seven sections and which takes several years, each gnome undergoes a process of maturing that I cannot express in words."

"Why not?"

"Simply because you are not gnomes!" he said, more sternly than usual. It was all very mysterious and rather disappointing, but it was useless arguing any further. We were obviously in front of a door the gnomes did not want to open for us because "something has to happen first."

How and why the gnomes had command of such a vast number of abilities that the rest of the world would probably never have, must remain a mystery. They had from time immemorial continued the pattern of behavior of the animals of the field together with the serenely applied use of Reason. As a result of the perfect harmony with the world around them, they did not experience any neuroses despite that application of the highest Reason. They did not pursue power or personal gain but achieved the ideal collectivism. They put into practice the law of Nature that dictates that the survival of the species is more important than the individual, and at the same time mastered the paradox that consciousness brings with it—all this for thousands of years without strife, self-interest, violence, or pollution.

It seemed as though we had been brought to Lapland to be shown where it all was and that it all existed, but we had been weighed and found too wanting to be allowed to take a real part in it.

It was a hard lesson.

"But," resumed Mirko, sensing our dejection, "much will depend on you in the coming weeks. There is enough time. Wait patiently even if it is not always pleasant. Anyway, what you have seen in the Secret Book will stand you in good stead during the coming trials. Draw accurately. Nicolas is not as bad as he seems. He will be a great help. Farewell!"

END OF THE FIRST PART

THE JOURNEY TO SIBERIA

Gradually we began to realize how everything fit to-gether. Mirko wanted us in Lapland to show us the Se-cret Book with its magic power during the midwinter period, but we would not be allowed to read it com-pletely this time. That was the lesson of the western gnomes.

At the same time Mirko would invite a Siberian gnome, whose tribe was clearly antagonized by the re-marks in our first book, to visit Lapland. This gnome would take us to Siberia. That was the lesson from the gnomes of the east. That was what we made of it.

It was decided that we would travel by a lemming-pulled troika. Our objective was the Yenisey River, about nineteen hundred miles ahead of us. We had dreaded the journey to Lapland but, compared with what we were about to undertake, that was child's play . . . and to think it was still winter and we were to be accompanied

by a grumpy gnome! Furthermore, it was an enigma as to how the little lemmings could undertake such a gigantic journey.

Siberia! Three times the size of Russia proper. Tem-peratures as low as −65° F. The taiga, an all-but-endless pine forest with floods and swamps; the tundras; the permafrost. The colossal rivers like the Yenisey, the Ob, the Lena, all unexpectedly flowing north, making it im-possible for the masses of melted ice in the south to flow away because the lower courses remain frozen, resulting in constant flooding. At last the moment had arrived. The troika stood in front of Elsa and Mirko's house with three strong East Russian lemmings ready to pull it.

Our luggage and book were on the sleigh, and we made our fond farewells. We did not, of course, want to give our real feelings away. We got in, and the troika shot off immediately.

We drew the heavy mammoth-hair rug over us. The animals found the way themselves. We gazed silently at the passing landscape. It was untouched and beautiful, even in the dark, but uncertainty gnawed at us and we wondered whether we would be able to stand the atrocious cold farther east. Nicolas did not utter a word and kept dozing off with intermittent snores. At regular intervals the lemmings stopped to rest and were given the grain Mirko had sent with us. The wind was mild and easterly.

The lemmings must have been dead tired by dawn, but they careened on, seemingly driven by something stronger than themselves. Sometimes they stopped to sniff the wind and then continued, barking, whining, and growling. Then, on a high plateau, they suddenly bolted. It was almost 10:00 A.M. The steep edge of the plateau came frighteningly near and we were afraid that we would be flung over the side, troika and all. Nicolas

sat up, drew his knife, and quick as lightning cut through the straps. While the lemmings disappeared before our eyes, over the side, the sleigh came to a halt exactly at the edge of the plateau. In the light of dawn we made out a brownish-white river far below us in the narrow valley. Soon we saw what it was: an endless stream of lemmings swarming eagerly southward. There must have been tens of thousands of them. We had hit upon the migration of the lemmings, which only happens once in five or eight years, and this one seemed exceptionally large.

Because of a number of favorable breeding years their numbers increase so rapidly that overpopulation results. Sometimes the females produce twelve offspring. The young of the first and second litter produce again within their first year, so that the increase via mathematical progression gets quite out of hand.

Normally they move from their winter abode in the mountains to the young spring grass of the lower reaches and return to the mountains in the autumn. In times of overpopulation the urge to migrate gets much stronger —away from the masses where sickness and famine lurk. The procession begins with tens but soon increases

to hundreds, thousands, and finally tens of thousands of lemmings.

Each animal has one goal: to get as far as possible, off to the horizon and even into glaciers. They cross rivers with ease, and even lakes, but finally they reach an ocean and, thinking this easy too, fling themselves in—sometimes from a great height—and drown en masse.

Needless to say, every animal or fish of prey helps to decimate the helpless columns.

It is touching to witness the courage of the little rodents: even against fox and wolf they adopt an aggressive attitude, balancing on their hind legs with backward-bent head.

Far below we saw our lemmings being admitted into the stream of animals. We lowered the troika over the edge of the plateau and hid it in the cleft of a rock. We took our luggage out and silently stared at Nicolas. That was the moment we heard the first friendly word from him: "Well done! No nagging about going back now?"

We started off for a forest on the far side of the valley and had to pass through the lemming column. For some reason we were not run over. Nicolas said, "They nearly all die. But it has been like that for centuries." He appeared to be less remote. It seemed as though his gruff manner was a bit put on. Soon we smelled a fox in the forest. Nicolas whistled hard on his fingers and in no time a penetratingly smelly white fox was standing before us. Nicolas whispered something in his ear. The fox agreed hesitatingly. "He will take us a good way east," said Nicolas, "although the rascal would rather go with the lemmings."

We jumped onto the back of the fox and held on tight to the deep, thick fur undercoat. We felt the rhythmical contracting and relaxing of the muscles under the supple skin during the fox's undulating gallop. The wind whistled through our hair.

Hours later Nicolas shouted "Stop!" Once we climbed down he sent the fox back on his own tracks. "That is to fool the trappers. Also I had to have him out of the way in connection with our accommodation tonight!"

The Arctic fox (Vulpes lagopus) *has a catlike appearance and dense fur. In summer it is an earth color; in winter it is as white as snow. One variation is the blue fox.*

We skied on a heathery plain interspersed with birch trees to an embankment with bushes, deep under snow. When Nicolas pushed aside a few branches, the entrance to a den was visible. He went in and spoke to someone far inside. Then he came back and said: "It's fine. We can stay here today. I shall introduce you to our host, a blackcock!"

We stuck the ends of our skis in the snow and went in. The blackcock looked at us fearlessly. He lifted one wing and we made ourselves comfortable against his warm body; then he draped his wing gently over us. We could feel his breathing and heartbeat but we were so tired that we soon fell asleep.

When we awoke it must have been evening. After our rest in the delicious feather bed we began to discuss the lemmings. Nicolas was nowhere as friendly as he had been that morning, but he did join in. "There are

Blackcocks making curving passages in the snow about three feet long. At the end there is a sitting room. Because of their high body temperature, a small air hole forms on the top of their head. Sometimes they spend an entire day in this den when their crop is full of heather and birch buds.

thousands of natural laws," he said, "against which we can do nothing. If an animal is in danger we are prepared to help him, as with the bear. But if it is a law of nature we can do nothing about it. The balance restores itself though it may seem cruel. One animal eats the other, but they never exterminate each other—only you do that. A lynx kills a roe deer for food. The sick, weak, and old are removed. That is not cruel, it is lack of compassion, which makes all the difference. It always makes sense. Only degenerate beings kill for nothing."

As we stood outside the den, the starry heavens stretched mightily above us. We put on our skis to explore the surrounding countryside. In some places the snow had been pushed aside and the heather below had been eaten. There were hollows smelling of animals just as deep in the snow as we had been. "Moose," mumbled Nicolas.

It was midnight by the time we returned to the den

of the blackcock. Instructed by Nicolas, we dug a square in the ground under the snow, lined it with flat stones, and lit a good fire. On leaving to find edible plants, he said: "Use the time to work on your book. I'll be back in a couple of hours."

When he returned with arms full of plants we made an earth oven.

Flat stones are placed in a square hole in the ground (don't use river stones—they explode!). A good fire can be kept burning for two hours on these stones. The glowing ashes are then spread out. Now the leathery leaves of the rock tripe (Umbilicaria) are spread on the stones. Over them goes a thick layer of the finer branches of reindeer moss (Cladonia ran-giferina), with wild onion bulbs (Allium) and rose hips (Rosa) on top. The next layer is more rock tripe, and then the whole thing is covered with a layer of earth.

Everything was cooked in an hour and the top layer of earth removed to reveal a steaming mass of vegetables before us. We consumed them at our leisure during the night.

Nicolas was grumpy but he poured us a generous acorn cup of fruit wine that he somehow had with him in spite of having left the troika behind. We were slowly beginning to appreciate him. "How could you find all those plants in the snow?" we asked.

"Reindeer moss grows everywhere. Wild onions are found below places where water collects. Those you can find without a divining rod, in folds of the ground. Rose hips hang above the snow, and can be found under it too, though they are somewhat damaged by the frost; nevertheless here they are."

Mother Earth was once more a tangible thing. You just had to have the feel for it.

To avoid getting scurvy in the long Arctic winters when there *are no green vegetables available, gnomes boil fir branches in* *water. The liquid contains just enough vitamin C to prevent the* *feared disease. As a result of lack of vitamin C hemorrhages* *occur in the muscles, under the periosteum of the long bones,* *and in the gums. If vitamin C is not administered in time, an* *extremely painful death follows. Another method is to drink the* *blood of a wolf or a dog, as these animals manufacture their own* *vitamin C. It is simpler to let the blood from the bast antlers of a* *reindeer, for it won't cause the animal to die. The bast antlers* *grow in early spring when the vitamin C content of the food is* *the lowest.*

Toward morning, our feathered host came into the open. His colors were a feast for the eye, but his eyes were gloomy.

"He is in trouble," said Nicolas. "There is a caper-caillie in the vicinity that not only disrupts all caper marriages, but also interferes with the ritual dance of the blackcocks. I think I shall have to do something about it."

Reindeer moss (Cladonia rangiferina)

"Can you?" we asked.

He frowned, whistled thoughtfully, and said, "Oh, very well then. I shall make an admission: I am a justice of the peace and I have to make decisions in all sorts of disputes. I am absolutely bound to appear wherever and whenever a complaint arises. I have set the session for seven o'clock tonight. First, let's get some sleep. Our host is too agitated to put us up now so we shall have to find another."

One heath farther we found a gray hen in the room. It was a sweet animal that sheltered us for the day as though we were her three chickens to be kept warm. We were so tired that we fell asleep immediately.

We awoke quite refreshed and, as we had the day before, chatted a bit; it was one of the gossips that we shall not forget for the rest of our lives. "Do you know why wild nature trails* always throw off light?" asked Nicolas. "It's because animals react to secret signs that elude people—for example, beams, magnetic waves,

and horizon changes. Perhaps humans were once able to perceive these things, but not anymore. A sled dog like the husky realizes from the color of the snow, a change of echo, a certain smell, an unusual tremor in the ice, and from great experience and instinct that a hidden fissure in the ice lays snow-covered in front of him, and he stops. Just try to copy that!"

We bid the gray hen adieu. She appeared grateful. Obviously she was honored and we had flattered her maternal feelings.

Meanwhile we were intrigued by the forthcoming court case. We skied after Nicolas to a wood on the horizon. There was already a snow-cleared area under the trees. In the middle was a round rock. Out of his suitcase Nicolas took a black gown with long white bands. Capercaillies were standing nearby and beyond them were some shy willow grouse and other onlookers.

* *A nature trail is a path frequented by wild animals.*

When Nicolas, adorned in his long toga, had taken his place on the stone, we heard the case of the blackcock, who was applauded by a whole group of capercaillies that had streamed in from all sides. Then came several capercaillie witnesses. It appeared that the capercaillie in question had gone much too far and could not leave the chickens alone. When the capercaillie gave his testimony it seemed to us that his defense was weak. Quite honestly, we did not think he was all there. We gained even more respect for Nicolas after hearing his questioning, which was conducted without any hurry. His command of the situation, his clear summing up, and especially his humor impressed us deeply. Secretly we agreed that he was the last person we would like to face if we had done something wrong.

When Nicolas had considered all the facts, he passed judgment. He denied the capercaillie, on penalty of having his wings clipped, the right to more than one hen per season and commanded him to abstain from all other disturbing activities, a decision that was received with loud applause from the audience. Thus the session was closed as there were no further complaints.

"Does he abide by your verdict?" we asked Nicolas.

"He better," he said severely. "I have my animal auxiliaries for this."

He changed into his normal clothes and we left. It was a cold and still Arctic night but we felt cozy. The snow squeaked softly under our skis and the clean, pure air filled our lungs. Hidden behind that gruff exterior Nicolas had a strong sense of justice and a good heart.

We realized that it was no accident that we had been sent to Siberia with this gnome but decided to ask him about it later anyway.

During a moment's pause we asked, "Do you get many such requests?"

"It never stops," he said. "The stream of complaints is endless. There are quarrels between animals, plants, stones, and even rivers about ownership, damage, theft, and dishonesty. Three of us control the area from Lapland as far as the Yenisey River, but we could use one more. I prefer to administer justice from a mushroom but with the snow of course there are none. My father and grandfather were both justices of the peace. We acquire the knowledge from each other, then we spend a couple of years at court to learn the fine points. My grandfather introduced the ruling that the badger and the fox could easily live together under one roof. The ruling that a roebuck, or for that matter any male animal, could chase an intruder from his territory up to and even a little be-

yond the boundary—but that aggression had to stop there—was introduced much earlier. This we enforce to the letter. My grandfather witnessed the case of the wolf and the fox: A wolf and a fox, both starving, saw a mare with her foal in a field. The fox sent the wolf to ask the mare if she would sell her foal, while he himself waited behind the fence. 'Certainly,' she said. 'Only I have completely forgotten the price. Would you look for yourself, Mr. Wolf? It is written under my right back hoof.' She lifted her hind leg for the wolf to see and gave him such a mighty kick that he lay unconscious for hours. The wolf then lodged a complaint against the fox for his trickery, and my grandfather had to deal with it. The wolf got no compensation or redress because he had willingly gone to the mare and should have been craftier, although my grandfather did give the fox a serious warning not to play such dirty tricks again."

While we were skiing along he continued: "Then there are the constantly recurring damage claims: trees complaining that rabbits gnaw on their roots or grub

them up; morning glories that strangle alders and willows; aggressive armies of ants that attack and devour everything in their path. There are complaints from the insect world about the red forest ants,* and so on. Last year a herd of red deer caused a rockslide that dammed a river. An area full of ground nesters was flooded just at breeding time. Luckily it was early spring so there was still time to build new nests. I sentenced each deer to protect three nests against predators and other menaces. The deer had to do so till the chickens were old enough to accompany their mothers. Naturally we got protests about this from foxes, martens, hedgehogs, crows, and

* *A red forest ant colony consists of about one million inhabitants and consumes one hundred thousand insects per day from the surrounding forest.*

magpies, but I ignored them. I deal regularly with bears that have stolen honey from a beehive. The bees approach me for damages because they can't do anything to the bears themselves. Bears are immune to bee stings except in the eye corners and the lips, but there he just wipes them away. Moreover, once it has stung a bee dies whereas a wasp doesn't. Above all, honey is the bees' foodstore for the winter. Naturally I'm talking about wild bees. They exist too, you know.

"The bear usually starts off with a denial, but in the face of twenty thousand witnesses he hasn't a leg to stand on. The only punishment I could impose would indeed be that the bear return the honey or at least sugar to the hive, but that is not easy in the wild. Usually such a bear gets away with a reprimand but I'm afraid I don't have many friends left among the bees."

The story of
Little Red Riding Hood and
the wolf can't be true.
Who would call a girl
Red Riding Hood
(and how could she appear
in one piece out of a wolf's
stomach), just to mention
a few discrepancies?

It's more likely that a
wolf with rabies ate a
she-gnome (with a pointed red cap)
by mistake.

Punch and Judy were
originally gnomes.
It happened like this:
Since olden days the gnomes,
as born actors, have given
their own shows at fairs
and annual markets,

and they have given
any money collected
to the poor.

Their wit and talent always stole
the show and caused professional
jealousy among bear owners, players,
quacks, fire-eaters, and magicians. That's why they
were expelled from their place in society in the
sixteenth and seventeenth centuries.

Naturally crafty chaps had long realized there was money to be made with this sort of entertainment.

They made hand puppets to imitate gnomes, thereby fooling simple people.

Over the years the gnomes' beard became the protruding chin of Punch and the pointed cap tilted foward.

Later, stupid tumbling toys and the insulting gnome pull toy were invented.

And the boring garden gnome

to lift his leg on...

It might only be used by an old dog

After Nicolas told us all this, we smelled a moose in the dense wood. In front of us we discovered a track; indeed it was difficult not to fall head over heels in the deep prints, and we had to bypass dung heaps as tall as we were.

The hoof mark of a bull moose is 4–6 inches long and 4–5 inches wide. The excrement is nearly as high as a gnome.

Moose and, to a lesser extent, Iceland ponies have an arched nose they use as a snowplow to collect food. The nostrils are placed fairly far back so that no snow can get in.

Finally we heard sniffing in front of us. We came across two bulls, one young and the other old. The older bull had lost his antlers. They towered above us with their enormous heads bowed to the ground. Nicolas spoke to them. It seemed less difficult than it was with the fox. "The older bull has just shed his antlers," our guide said. "That makes a difference of forty pounds. He will take us part of the way."

An hour later we were storming through field and forest at a great height with the wind whistling in our ears. The young moose had come along too. The older one, upon whose head we sat, was careful to see that we were not whisked off by passing branches. Their long-legged trot could evidently be kept up for hours. They stopped toward morning, promising to return later to take us a little farther. After they left, Nicolas explained: "Moose do not have a permanent home. They roam. They travel hundreds of miles in the mating season."

While we were searching for a blackcock's hole we noticed a straight line of small trees. "Those were planted by gnomes," Nicolas said, "to enable them to cross from one hiding place to another without being seen."

Within a quarter of an hour we had found a blackcock's spoor, and after a number of U-turns, doubling back, circles, and other peculiar maneuvers, it ended at a hole.

We followed the same procedure as we had before.

While Nicolas was away looking for food we kept warm by the earth oven and worked on the book, which had been wrapped and placed at the bottom of our knapsack. A magic spell seemed to flow from it just by holding it, and while leafing through the entries we had made, we were conscious of all sorts of intangible things around us.

After supper we once again crept "under wing" and slept soundly till evening. We felt we were one with life on earth.

Our appreciation of each other increased as it is often apt to do when people are thrown together. That evening, upon waking under the wing, Nicolas even muttered, "So, old chaps, slept well?"

Our conversation touched on plant life. "Naturally a plant registers what goes on around him or her," said

Nicolas. "It has a primeval perceptive faculty that existed among living cells long before the five senses. It is not bound by time or space. Something happens of which one is simply part. A tree experiences being chopped down as a human would experience being led to the gallows. It is odd that you people have such a considerable knowledge of the workings of the heart and brain, aided only by weak electric currents, and yet you are deaf to these plant signals!"

The moose returned the following evening. The east wind had become a strong west wind. Nicolas rubbed his hands together as he looked at the sky and mumbled, "We can soon travel faster!"

"Do you mean by bird?"

"Just wait patiently!" he said mysteriously.

By morning the moose had done forty miles. We alighted, thanked them, and sent them back. We were on a wooded slope.

In the moonlight we noticed a cave dug into the side of the hill. Nicolas shouted a few unintelligible words as we drew near, whereupon there was a sound of yawning and shuffling. To our horror, a broad-shouldered troll appeared. Nicolas gestured to us reassuringly and said, "So, Cork. Everything all right?"

For sheer joy at seeing Nicolas, the troll began to jump up and down with his flailing flat feet. "Shake hands with my friends," commanded Nicolas.

Cork wiped his hands under his armpits and offered us a greasy, bristly troll hand. "Is everything ready?" Nicolas asked.

The troll nodded emphatically and we entered a short passageway leading to a large space where a night-light was glowing and, of all things, a balloon was hanging from the ceiling. We stared incredulously.

"Quite so. A balloon," said Nicolas. "Made from the bladder of a mammoth. It contains fifty-three cubic feet of natural gas."

"A mammoth bladder?"

"Yes. There are still plenty of mammoths to be found in the permafrost. It takes one slash in the abdomen, bladder out, abdomen closed. Then wash, salt, and dry the bladder. It is then so elastic it can be blown up to many times its original size."

"And the gas?"

"Our good friend Cork gets that out of the ground. He has improved so much that he can say twelve words without one mistake. He is paid in food and gold to have a balloon ready here at all times. Between here and the Yenisey River we have three such trolls. This is Cork I. We have Cork II, Cork III, and finally Crown Cork; one every five hundred miles."

Cork grinned broadly at these words. Bellows hung on the wall. There were balloon baskets of woven reed, a couple of nets, and an empty reserve balloon.

"Cork can mend nets and repair baskets now," said Nicolas. "He even is house-trained. It has taken years."

"Where does the gas come from?"

"Deep in the ground. It is a slow process, bellow by bellow, but Cork has oceans of time. There are still ancient reserves stored up by the gnomes."

"Tonight we take off, Cork," Nicolas said to the obediently listening troll with arms hanging at his sides. "See that everything is in order and get a blanket for us."

The blanket Cork took from a wall cupboard smelled fresh, as if it had been plunged into a mountain stream.

Nicolas took hard-baked biscuits and nuts from another cupboard and made tea on a primitive stove. He slept on the blanket after supper but we got caught up in our book, which we managed to work on without getting cold fingers. After three hours we too went to sleep; Nicolas was snoring beside us. Cork lay in a corner on a bed of fir branches. The balloon cast huge shadows on the ceiling. It was eerie.

When we awoke, Nicolas had three plates of steaming porridge ready that he had sprinkled liberally with sugar. The balloon had disappeared and there was a sound outside of falling gravel.

"Cork puts pebbles in the basket as ballast," said Nicolas. "We will leave as soon as we have eaten."

When we went out, the balloon looked even bigger. "Cork has put in a bit more gas," said Nicolas. "When it is completely full it won't fit through the passageway. It's now twelve and a half times lighter than air."

In one hand Cork held a rope and with the other he was throwing pebbles into the basket, which also contained a blanket.

The net was neatly draped over the balloon and attached to the basket by the string ends. Nicolas threw in a bag of nuts and dried mushrooms and said, "Well done, Cork. I'm satisfied."

We stepped in while Cork held on to the balloon. As he eased off the ropes, the balloon rose ten feet, and we

jumped up and down and stamped as directed by Nicolas, just like experienced balloonists.

"Is everything ready?" asked Nicolas, a bit out of breath from stamping. "Here we go then! Let go, Cork!"

A troll that walks into a gnome trap is set free after a few days (the days are counted by undoing one knot per day from a knotted rope). Sometimes the troll must spend a few extra days on a rock in the middle of a river . . . a troll cannot swim and is therefore terrified of water. Most trolls return to the forest swearing and cursing without improving a bit, but it does sometimes happen that a troll repents. If his intelligence seems any higher than other trolls', he is trained as a balloon-ready holder. The gnomes make the balloon, rigging, and basket, but the troll has to keep it ready for use filled with gas.

On the following pages are various traps used to overpower trolls.

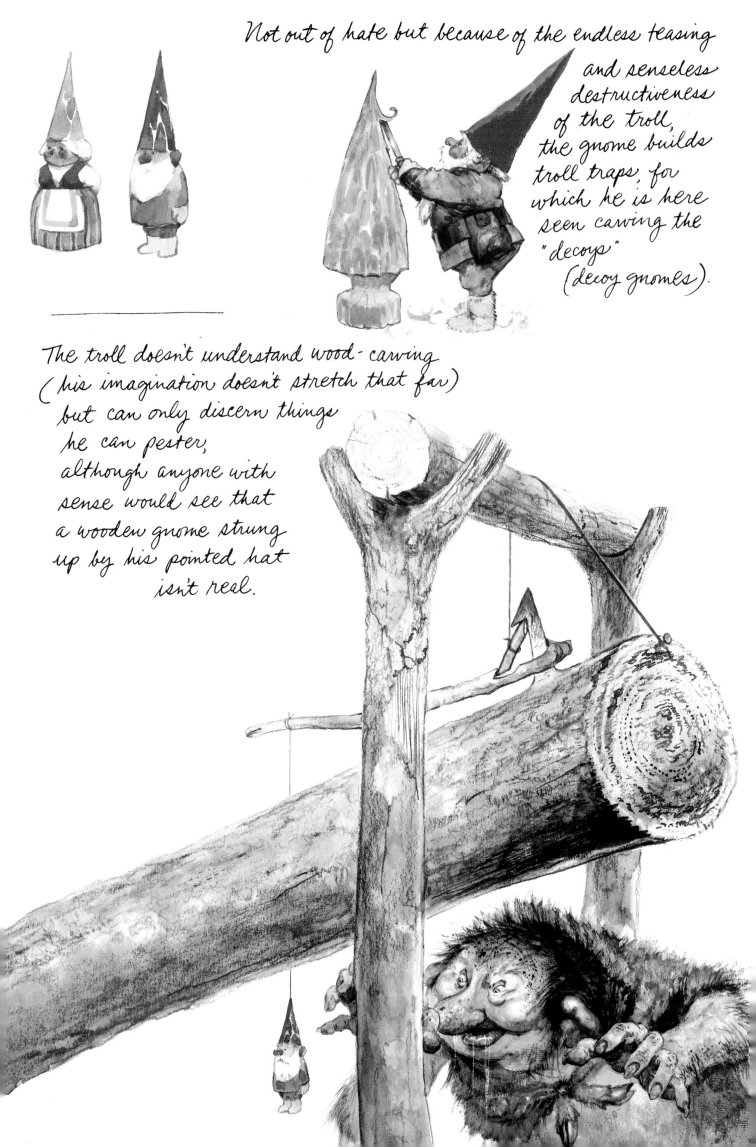

Not out of hate but because of the endless teasing and senseless destructiveness of the troll, the gnome builds troll traps, for which he is here seen carving the "decoys" (decoy gnomes).

The troll doesn't understand wood-carving (his imagination doesn't stretch that far) but can only discern things he can pester, although anyone with sense would see that a wooden gnome strung up by his pointed hat isn't real.

Once in the trap, the troll pulls the door closed behind him and remains there trotting in an endless circle — for lack of any constructive thinking — until he is freed by the gnome.

Even the simplest trap principle is a sure success!

Whether a flower, mushroom, or a brood of eggs
is concerned — no matter what —
the troll rushes at it
with but one thought
in mind:

SQUASH IT!

SQUASH IT!

The FIST-PUNISHER is based on this squasher
principle :
　　　　　it packs a hefty punch,
　　　　　　and even when the axle is
↙　　　　　　frozen stiff in icy
　　　　　　　weather the sharpened
　　　　　　　　wooden cap comes
　　　　　　　　　into its own.

↓

There are many variations on a theme: decoy gnome and charging idiot.

The punishment element speaks for itself!

In spite of everything, the gnome still shows compassion for the troll!

The so-called
WRIST-TRAP
is made in an
old woodpecker's hole. →

No sooner does the red
pointed hat inside
catch the eye of our
dirty friend

than, grab-bang,
the wrist goes
in
↓

and the
silence of
the
forest
is rudely broken by
screams and curses.

———

Anything colorful
that <u>dares</u> to
appear <u>has</u>
to be <u>broken</u>.

As soon as the infant trolls are born they start kicking
around blindly. Only the meanest kicker remains alive,
sometimes one out of a nest of five.
The yelping victims do not even cause the mother to turn around.
Senseless destruction of a bird is obviously more interesting.

Gnomes protect their homes adequately against retaliation
by the trolls by making a signpost with
the arrow pointing the wrong way.
_____
Friends and trusted visitors just know
they have to go the other way.

(travelogue continued)

The balloon surged up about a hundred feet and was caught by the wind. Below us the forest passed by quickly while the balloon continued to rise. It was probably terribly cold outside but it didn't worry us. After a while we didn't notice the wind either, because we were traveling just as fast. The air was still. Nicolas held a cord connected to a valve that would let gas out of the balloon when we wanted to descend.

"My guess is that the wind is about twenty-two miles per hour," he said. "If we keep on like this we will reach Cork II in twenty-four hours. Anything could happen . . . the wind could slow or change course!"

Everything was going according to plan. We kept pace with the clouds above us, flying at a height of about three hundred and fifty feet. At one point we had to clear a high hill, which necessitated throwing a couple of handfuls of pebbles overboard. We saw a herd of deer now and then and a solitary bear. Once trolls pelted stones at us but there was no danger of our being hit.

The endless forest was broken here and there by cultivated fields or a village, but no one saw us and we floated thirteen hundred feet high without interference because, Nicolas said, that was the best height to avoid opposing air currents.

It snowed toward morning and the balloon soon had

a cap of snow, so we once again had to unload some stones. "We shall have to fly on during the day," said Nicolas. "Luckily the area between the rivers Onega and Severnay is thinly populated." We cracked some nuts and ate dried mushrooms in fruit wine. It was a mystery to us where Nicolas got all that drink.

Dusk fell and we again drifted into the night.

Toward morning we saw a reddish glow on the eastern horizon. "The industrial zone of Syktyvkar," said our guide. "We have to go beyond it. There is an airport. Let's hope they don't spot us."

Fortunately the balloon was too small to be detected by their radar. Or they thought it was a child's balloon.

Or the air-controllers were napping. In any event we glided over without any trouble, although every now and then the air was full of suffocating smoke and we saw the fiery glow of the ovens directly below us.

There was still a strong wind as the clouds began to break. Nicolas looked at the stars and grunted contentedly. He pulled on the gas-outlet string and there was a hiss. The earth approached slowly. As the treetops sped past increasingly nearer, Nicolas made us jettison all the stones so that we rose somewhat. He let out more gas above a deep river valley and the balloon descended at an oblique angle to the frozen river behind the shelter of the hill.

Once down we stretched our stiff legs and wandered about a bit. Then we put on skis and went off. Within half an hour we reached a small house built on a sawed-off fir trunk with a ladder leaning against it. A small troll who appeared more intelligent than Cork I appeared in the doorway. He looked unhappy.

"Is everything all right?" Nicolas asked.

"No," said the troll. "Old comrades been here."

"What is broken?"

"Everything. Leak in balloon. Net torn. Basket stolen. Food eaten. Me hit and kicked!"

We climbed up and examined the damage. Cork II lifted up a balloon full of holes.

Nicolas walked around grunting and furiously kicked the pieces of ruined net in the air. "They will pay for this!" he said. "Who were they?"

The balloon troll on duty has a weather vane to indicate which way the wind is blowing and thus which way the balloon will go. In addition, the weather vane provides company for the troll, and gives him the happy feeling that a friend is there, helping him day and night, to whom he can wave and speak, and whom he has to protect against other trolls.

"Stamp, Gnash, and Fist. Far away now!"

"I'll get them," said Nicolas. "Will you fetch our balloon? It is a little way upstream, on this side."

Cork II disappeared with the speed of a beast of prey.

Nicolas said, "We must use our own balloon again. But filling it with gas takes a couple of days."

We had nuts and mushrooms for one more meal and then went to sleep. Meanwhile Cork had returned with the balloon and basket, but had left again by the time we awoke. "He is fetching gas," said Nicolas, "from a deep cleft in the earth where we have been getting it for centuries."

While Nicolas was away looking for vegetables, Cork appeared periodically with bellows of gas. As soon as Nicolas returned we made another earth oven. Then we climbed up into the house and spent half the night talking about the climate behind the Urals, and other things. We drew as much as we could in the book and fell asleep toward morning. Cork shuffled back and forth outside. He had to be careful of the daylight, as direct sun rays turn a troll to stone.

We were awakened by Cork's proud announcement at the top of the ladder: "Balloon ready!" It was pitch black outside. The balloon was hanging high up in the air. Cork gave Nicolas a huge sack. He looked in it and said, "Well, what do you know—hazelnuts! Where did you find these?"

"Fetched them," said Cork. "From far! For Nicolas."

"Good troll," said Nicolas with great appreciation. "You will get an honorable mention."

After this we skied away to collect reindeer moss, and Nicolas showed us how to find it in the snow. We returned an hour and a half later. Nicolas said to Cork once more: "I am really very satisfied. You have done exceptionally well," whereupon Cork turned scarlet and wiped his nose on his upper right arm.

We were soon rising above the trees in our basket. The wind blew the balloon above us obliquely eastward and before long we were swinging calmly in a moderate breeze about eight hundred feet above the endless waves of forest landscape.

We did one hundred twenty-five miles at the beginning of the evening, until the wind increased our speed; it got colder. The next sixty miles went one and a half times as fast. The icy air filled our eyes, and icicles formed on our mouths and noses. Nicolas looked anxiously at the sky. "We are getting into a storm," he said, "but I want to take advantage of our speed for as long as possible." Squalls tossed the basket and balloon backward and forward. Our speed rose alarmingly. Nicolas made us jettison stones in the belief that the squalls would be less severe at a higher altitude, which luckily proved to be correct.

The landscape below flew by at a tremendous speed as the storm increased in strength. We had to scream to make ourselves heard and felt terribly uncomfortable, but we made enormous progress. Nicolas remained calm.

Toward morning the sky lightened to a yellow-gray. It was abominably cold, we were exhausted, and the storm had increased to a hurricane. Finally Nicolas shouted, "The wind is veering to the south. We must go down or we will be blown off course."

We sighed with relief. To be safely on the ground among solid trees or in a cave seemed like it would be heaven after this terrifying storm. But when Nicolas pulled the rope to let the gas escape, nothing happened. The valve was stuck! We all pulled on the rope to no avail. The balloon was lifted now by the hurricane and in fits and starts we went higher and higher. Sometimes the hurricane seemed to be aiming direct blows at us. Nicolas climbed in the rigging. When he was back in the basket he shouted, "The valve is frozen shut with ice. Nothing can be done about it. We'll just have to make the best of it!"

The next twelve hours passed in a stupor. Dawn broke, eclipsed by heavy, dark clouds. One moment there was sleet, then snow. There were no longer forests below us; plains stretched as far as the eye could see. We must have been blown far to the north. Our limbs were

stiff and our only solace was from the drink and nuts provided by Cork II. We were exhausted from the constant swinging of the basket, to say nothing of our anxiety about the whole ordeal. We must have done six hundred miles. We were heading toward the Arctic Ocean when the hurricane lost some of its fury. Then, however, the ominous black clouds erupted—snow first, then hail. (Remember, a hailstone to a gnome is as big as his foot!) Most of the hailstones hit the balloon but some struck us like bricks. Above us sledgehammer blows rained on the balloon. Suddenly Nicolas pushed up his earflaps. We heard hissing. He pointed upward and shouted, "The balloon is leaking!"

The swollen balloon had not been able to withstand the drumming blows of the hailstones. We began to de-scend and quickly plunged at an angle to the ground that we had been longing for during the last hours. It would be a hard landing. We hit the ground in a cloud of snow and the basket bounced. Finally, after being hurled across the snowy plain, the balloon came to a standstill near the banks of the frozen Arctic Ocean. The hailstorm had stopped. We got out, stiff and numb. Nicolas said, "We can't stay here. We must get to the snow peaks on the other side, where we can build an igloo or perhaps find a polar bear's den. Right now I need to find mud. There must be soil so near the bank." He cut a square of ice loose. "We will tie that behind the basket," he said. "Then we will stay on course." We helped him enlarge the hole in the ice until we dug through to the earth, about one and a half feet deep.

Just as the Eskimos do with the underside of their sleighs, he rubbed the bottom of our skis with mud, let it freeze, wet it again, and then smoothed it with his knife to get a glossy surface. We then tied the skis side by side under the basket while Nicolas attached the ice block. We folded the balloon, stepped in the basket, and gave the whole thing a push with the ski poles till it was swept forward by the wind. We could maneuver by steering the ice block to the left or right. For the moment we thought the worst had passed.

The basket slid effortlessly over the vast expanse of ice, which was in itself a pleasant feeling, though we couldn't help wondering how we were ever going to get back to Holland. Three hours later, when we finally reached a high cliff of ice on the other side of the frozen estuary, we could find no trace of a polar bear. "We'll have to build an igloo," Nicolas said.

Building an igloo: wedge-shaped blocks are cut from the ice with a snow saw. Rings of ice blocks are placed in a spiral until the top of the round building is completed. The builder stands inside. The final piece at the center top is a block of ice with an air hole in it. When the builder is finished he hacks a low passage to the outside and makes a roof over it. A well-built igloo never collapses and is only rendered stronger by a slight sagging. All openings are closed off by an extra layer of snow.

When the igloo was ready we pulled the balloon inside. There was plenty of room to sleep on it and we turned up the edges as a sort of blanket. Without fuel for a fire we had to eat the reindeer moss raw. Our problems dominated our thoughts. We were sheltered for the moment but this situation could not go on indefinitely. Nicolas was buried in thought. At last he said: "Let's sleep first. After that I'll leave to find help—alone!"

"What about us?" we asked. "Must we stay here alone?"

"You are safe here. The snow will quench your thirst—let it melt slowly in your mouth. There are still some nuts and reindeer moss. I'll be back in three or four days—I can go faster on my own. I'll leave some brandy."

"What about you?"

He slapped his stomach with his broad hand and laughed, "I can easily go for days on snow and nuts!"

We watched sadly as he left at noon, but realized that his iron constitution was well suited for feats of en-

durance. The loneliness of the igloo became unbearable after a few hours. We needed exercise and the best thing to do was to get out and ski. As long as we kept sight of the ice cliff, it was practically impossible to get lost. There was no wind and because we were on the move we were able to keep fairly warm in spite of our insufficient clothing. The landscape was monotonous. We felt hungry and ate a nut. Would we be able to see the renowned northern lights? They were reputed to be soft green and violet; for the present we saw nothing. We were amazed at the distance even the slightest sound traveled.

Suddenly we noticed two specks ahead of us on the ice, one large and one small. As we approached we discovered that they were seals, a mother with her pup; they had crept onto the ice from their breathing hole. Perhaps we could cadge a fish from them! Gnomes might be vegetarians but that didn't have to apply to us. And who could say when Nicolas would return? We considered fish a welcome complement to our meager menu.

The seals were not frightened of us—we must have been gnome enough—they just gazed at us with bulging eyes. The pup was a darling. When we asked the mother if she would catch us a fish she said nothing but stared over our heads into the distance. Obviously she could not quite place a request like this from a gnome. We would have to catch one for ourselves. At least she didn't object to our using her hole for this.

We returned to the hole two hours later, having made a hook from the pin in a belt buckle and a line from string on the balloon. We chewed up a hazelnut, put the resulting concoction on the hook, and froze it. We then placed it gingerly in the hole. There was no trace of the seals. Since we didn't have a float we had to keep pulling up the line at the slightest movement. Nothing was happening—the fish were either asleep or not at home. Sometimes the bait disintegrated in the water. We sat next to the hole for hours, getting unbearably cold. Now and then the seals would surface in our hole or the neighboring hole, which naturally scared the fish away.

Hours and hours passed without any luck until at last there was a flailing resistance in the depths. Thrilled, we both clung to the line. It must be a giant fish. We let him tire before pulling him in, afraid that he would escape from the slippery makeshift hook. We succeeded in getting him onto the ice: a flounder seven inches long! Food for days. We slapped each other proudly on the back. We killed the flounder immediately to save its suf-

fering unnecessarily and went back to the igloo, dragging the fish behind us on the line. It got misty but we could keep the cliff in view.

At one point we happened to look behind us and froze with fright. An enormous monster was following us. It was the size of an elephant but had a long tail and a huge panting mouth full of teeth. It appeared to be close behind us, and we fully expected it to charge at any moment. Blind with fear we made for the protection of the cliff; perhaps we could find a place to hide. The monster followed us with huge leaps. In fact it should already have been upon us. We dropped the fish and crept behind a ledge in the cliff. A wedge of ice fell with a loud

thud behind us; at that moment the monster vanished. We looked across the ice plain and saw an Arctic fox approaching in the distance. He was following the scent of the fish with his nose to the ice. We climbed down quickly and waited by the flounder for the fox to reach us. He lifted his head, put his nose in the air to get our scent, and looked disbelievingly from the fish to us and back, but he didn't take the fish.

We stood face to face like this for some time. Eventually he turned and trotted off and we pulled our forthcoming meal to the igloo. We lashed the fish under the upturned balloon basket behind the igloo. Then we went inside, ate half a nut each, and fell into a deep sleep.

It was evening when we awoke and we crawled to the outside. The flounder had not been touched. Apparently there were no more foxes or polar bears in the vicinity. We each hacked off a generous piece from the solidly frozen fish and took them inside. Frozen raw flounder turned out to be a delicacy. We ate copious amounts of it, swilling it down with brandy, and peacefully fell asleep again. The next day we went for a little ski trip on the lake in order to loosen our muscles and to get rid of our headaches.

Our routine was the same during the next twenty-four hours. Nicolas had been gone for almost three days, but we would be able to hold out for another week with our freezer fish. It was cold and misty and sometimes razor-sharp ice crystals formed in the air.

As we were taking another short trip in the gloomy daylight we suddenly saw something that made us freeze in our tracks: there, over the ice, a huge Santa Claus was approaching. We stood still and watched him in fear and amazement. Like the monster we saw the

previous day, he seemed to be right in front of us. Again, we couldn't hear him and he didn't seem to be getting any closer. We hurried back to the igloo and when we looked around, Santa Claus was gone. A gust of wind had dispersed the mist and the large icefield stretched out clearly before us. Far away in the distance a tiny dot was approaching, and fifteen minutes later it proved to be Nicolas. He was carrying a big parcel. When he had put his baggage down we embraced him and told him about the monster and Santa Claus. He burst out laughing and said: "You've seen nothing more than a fox and me. Haven't you ever heard of light refraction? When there is a certain degree of humidity in the air, it causes small objects at the horizon to grow into gigantic shapes; it is a kind of mirage. But I have good news. A day and a half's journey from here is a settlement of Arctic gnomes. We have to get there as quickly as possible, because there is another snowstorm on its way. We will only take what we can carry. First, you have to put on these clothes that our Arctic brothers have provided us with."

He had all kinds of things with him: sealskin boots (the inner and outer soles were separated by a thin layer of dried grass); hare-wool socks; a shirt made of bird skin with down on the inside; a shiny pair of white pants made of sheared hare fur, which tucked into the boots. It all was topped by a beautiful, loosely fitting coat of sheared hare fur, with a deep fur hood attached that served as the pointed hat, and a pair of kid gloves. We felt like princes.

"But now I have to rest for a few hours because I am exhausted."

We entered the igloo, prepared a meal of flounder

and nuts, and poured out a drink to celebrate our re-union in this barren country. Nicolas ate it all with gusto, including the fish! Then he lay down and slept soundly for five hours. Later he opened his eyes, got up, and said: "Let's go!"

We made our way along the high ice wall, climbing over it at a low point, and arrived on a vast icefield. The first part of the journey was terrible. Thousands of ice points and crevasses made skiing almost impossible. Sometimes Nicolas saw, in the same way as Arctic dogs can, hidden crevasses under the snow where we wouldn't have suspected anything; in order to get around them we had to backtrack for long distances. The frozen mud had broken off our skis completely. After many hours we began to descend and finally reached smoother ice with patches of snow.

The origin of the belief in Santa Claus can be explained as follows: in the wintry cold and snowy skies, the light refraction caused people from time to time to see ordinary gnomes who had taken on giant proportions.

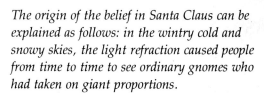

While we were resting we asked Nicolas, "Where do Arctic gnomes get their fur from? They don't kill animals or eat meat or fish, do they?"

"Here they do eat them and use their fur," he said, "but they don't kill them. The gnomes have to rely on them because there is nothing else. They take what they need from the Arctic fox's winter store; the fox doesn't object, especially as gnomes don't need much."

Twelve hours later we approached another ice cliff. We could see igloos in the distance. The next minute a bunch of fur-clad gnomes were clicking toward us on snowshoes. They emitted wild cries and practically knocked us over embracing us, rubbing noses, and pinching us amicably. At the igloos we were about to creep in through the tunnel when a sort of letter opener was thrust at us for brushing off snow and ice particles from our fur clothing that might melt and then freeze again later with serious consequences.

This illustrates how small such a gnome igloo is.

The brushing of clothes can take up considerable time after journeys in snowstorms, and meanwhile it gives the one who enters time to call "Someone has arrived!"–thus assuring the observance of good manners.

The cone shape of a gnome cap serves to prevent his being flattened by loads of snow or other disasters from above, because objects simply glance off the sides.

We crept farther into the tunnel. Dexterous hands pulled our anoraks over our heads. We were in the main igloo around which the other smaller ones were built. The smaller ones were connected to the main one by tunnels so that the inhabitants could contact each other without going outside.

We were barely inside when the snowstorm prophesied by Nicolas broke in full force. A smoky fire was burning in the igloo. The few women inside had on nothing more than short pants, which startled us at first, but it was obviously the norm here. Quite soon the men undressed entirely. Two of them dragged legs of snow hare onto the platform of the igloo. It was apparent that they were preparing a party for us. The meat was boiled in pots and seal bacon bubbled in other vessels.

The men were smaller than us. They had black eyes and very black greasy hair. All had broad, oval faces. The women laughed constantly while they rapidly prepared the food with their small, well-shaped hands.

The large igloo was the meeting place for eating and dancing, and the gnome families apparently lived in the smaller igloos.

While we were waiting for the meal Nicolas said, "I will give you the basic rules for survival in the wilderness:

1. Water is always more important than food.
2. In intense cold always breathe through your nose, never through your mouth.
3. In extreme circumstances you can go without sleep for five days.
4. Travel in the late night hours and in early morning.
5. Panic is your worst enemy. With normal reserves you can withstand hunger, thirst, cold, heat, loneliness, fatigue, long distances, physical injury, and loss of blood for a long period. Panic always upsets the balance. Remain calm. Make the most of every situation.
6. If you have to undertake something, consider whether you: react quickly . . . or recklessly; are cautious . . . or only frightened; demand enough . . . or too much of yourself and others.
7. See to it that you are armed against scurvy in perpetual snow areas by daily drinking water in which pine twigs have been boiled. Take them along with you into icy areas.
8. Remember that snow is an excellent insulator. Look how sled dogs let themselves get snowed under right up to the tips of their noses (which they then cover with their bushy tails).
9. Frostbite begins with numbness. Pay attention to that. A frozen patch turns gray or whitish-yellow. Don't rub it! You'll break the skin. Warm your limb under your arm or thaw it in lukewarm water.
10. To orient yourself:
    Clouds above open water are dark gray,
    clouds above snow or ice are white,
    birds fly early in the morning from the land to the sea
    and in the evening from the sea to land
    (seagulls, puffins, and hunters).

This is all in the Secret Book!" he said. He showed it to us, as well as illustrations of a Yeti family and gnomes from far-off places.

Yeti, front view   Yeti, from behind

These are in fact
actual pictures of the
YETI or ABOMINABLE SNOWMAN

(which he doesn't want to exist at all!)
and he is a grand master at not being seen.

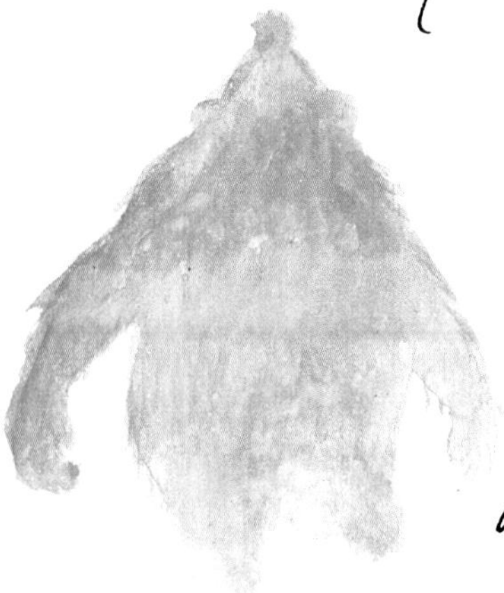

He is reproduced on the opposite page with
unnatural clarity.

This will give you
an idea of
the difference
in
body size:

Yeti   Homo sapiens   gnome

The ABOMINABLE SNOWWOMAN,
in spite of her superfluous milk
supply, switches rapidly to an
additional feeding for her small
Yeti (abominable snowchild)
of ice wafers, water ices,
ice creams, and frost
flowers, etc.

The Yeti normally walks upright.
If he thinks he is being observed he walks on all fours.

This is why Arctic and Himalayan travelers have for centuries thought that what they saw was a polar bear.

He glides over frozen lakes at enormous speeds.

When we were finally seated in a circle and about to begin the meal, the oldest gnome said that he hoped we were not too hungry because the meat was of an inferior quality, actually not fit to set before guests, more like dog meat. Nicolas appeared to be au fait with the rules of the game as he immediately said that we were certainly not hungry and had just dropped by for the company. The old gnome cut a slice of meat, tasted it, chewed it, and said: "Just as I said—worthless meat, half-rotten and badly prepared. I don't dare to give it to you!" He had barely uttered the words when everyone dove into the food. Deep into the night we devoured the finest legs of hare and legs of duck, and then alternated with seal bacon. The criticism of the food was a sort of courtesy ritual. We glistened with grease from head to toe and could hardly utter a word. During the meal we had heard numerous stories about living in snow and ice that only increased our respect for these friendly, cheerful gnomes who considered hospitality their ultimate duty.

It turned out that although everyone was happily naked, the clothes Nicolas had brought for us were the same as theirs. Finally we went off to bed. We were each allotted a separate small igloo, and not without reason: two husbands put their wives at our disposal as a generous gesture, a custom that one could not refuse at this latitude without offending someone, so we left it at that.

The storm was still raging when we awoke. We were assured that it would last three or four days, and there was no chance of journeying farther. We spent the days chatting, listening to old tales, and watching how the Arctic gnomes ran their households. As a toy they use a *snorrebot:* a piece of bone or button with two holes is threaded with two strings. Once it gets going it keeps whirring around as long as the threads are rhythmically extended and retracted.

Seeing the women sewing fur was fascinating. They cut pieces from a skin with a small knife that had a handle in the center. Tanning was done by chewing the hide. The pieces were assembled without any measuring and were sewn together with a bone needle and a thread of walrus hide. When it was ready no seam was evident in the shorn fur, and the garment was always a perfect fit. Precision in sewing together the fur pieces is of vital importance as a split seam can let so much cold through in a storm that frostbite might result.

We spent the days reading their Secret Book and getting ours up to date. The storm did indeed begin to abate after the third day. On the fourth day it was suddenly absolutely still. We all went outside and had a

good stretch. This time we were lucky: blue and violet streaks adorned the evening sky and yellow-green and soft reddish tints marked the horizon. The famous northern lights (aurora borealis), which occur because sun-born electrons and protons bombard the oxygen and nitrogen molecules in our atmosphere, revealed themselves in all their beauty.

Suddenly we noticed that the gnomes seemed to be looking at something we could not see. Nicolas stood beside us and laughed: "There goes our lift to Cork III!"

When we looked at him inquiringly, he said, "Look carefully! Don't you see anything?"

We peered intently. After a long time we saw a vague shape. "Quite!" said Nicolas. "That is a Yeti."

"But aren't they only found in the Himalayas?"

"There are more of them in the world than you think. They can make themselves invisible; no human has ever seen one."

The oldest gnome had come to stand next to us. "Would you ask the Yeti if he could take us to Cork III?" asked Nicolas. We skied behind the old gnome toward the body disappearing in the distance and in half an hour we had caught up with him.

The Yeti stood still. The old gnome bowed and said, "Good evening, Zero. Haven't seen you for a long time. How is Frigida and little Ice Cream?"

The gigantic figure made no reply and regarded us suspiciously. Eventually he said in a deep voice, "Those look like two people. Are you sure I won't risk being discovered?"

"I guarantee that personally," said the Arctic gnome, while Nicolas growled in our ear: "They have one-track minds—fear of being seen."

"All right then," said Zero, "although I don't relish taking risks."

A quarter of an hour later we had reached an agreement: he would take us to Altay, five hundred miles to the southeast, the following evening.

"And I don't want you to see how I walk,'" he said, "even though you are gnomes. I have an old blanket at home and you'll go into that."

He stuck to his words. He came rumbling along the following evening carrying a grayish-red blanket. A long farewell to the gnomes then took place while Zero spread the blanket on the ice. When we eventually stood on the blanket, Nicolas said, "Where did you get this blanket? It seems familiar!"

"I found it a hundred years ago as I was on the way home from north Tibet, after visiting my nephews and nieces in the Himalayas."

"Good Lord," said Nicolas, "that is one of Nikolai Przhevalsky's blankets. He has indeed been to north Tibet . . . I'll tell you about it on the way."

Zero pulled the blanket around us and held it by the four corners so we sat in a cozy hole. We were at his mercy. "Nothing to fear," said Nicolas. "Yetis are absolutely reliable." It was pitch black in the blanket and it didn't smell terribly fresh. We seemed to be traveling at a high speed. "Yes, old Przhevalsky," said Nicolas. "I saw him enter Mongolia from Kyakhta in November 1871. He was a tough, testy rascal, and he traveled with camels. He stayed in Mongolia for three years and came as far as north Tibet. That was where his camels gave out from exhaustion. It so happened that I was there and slept in his tent. We could not get fresh camels so on my advice he switched to yaks. A yak is a mountain creature without parallel. It can go to an altitude of twenty thousand feet and can follow mountain paths with a burden of 250 pounds beside precipices even difficult for mountain goats and sheep—all without one slip of a hoof.

"Przhevalsky* had to return because of a lack of funds. He was the one who discovered the horse that is named after him, and the wild camel. He must have lost this blanket somewhere on the way.

"This is in any case a strange way of traveling! We gnomes have other means of transport."

The wild yak lives at altitudes up to twenty thousand feet. The bull weighs up to 2,000 pounds, the cow 880. Hair: long blackish-brown. Tame yak: bull up to 1,500 pounds, cow 770. Color: light to spotted. Milk: thick and creamy. Yaks can be ridden. In snowstorms they remain so still that they appear dead.

yak

Przewalski paard

* Nikolai M. Przhevalsky, 1839–1888, Russian general. Made four voyages of discovery through Asia and Tibet, and charted part of it.

Nicolai Michailowitsch Przewalski

Troika, elk, and Arctic fox
are not the only
means of transportation!

When weather conditions
are propitious, the gnomes
make fifteen-mile night marches
on foot,

easily taking in stride the load
of a sled filled with nuts

↓

↙ or of a wood chick.
The old knapsack and the
basket filled with
fruit, which they
carry on their backs,
don't slow them down
at all.

For quick shopping trips, they use the walking bicycle (eleven thousand years old),

↓   and for slow trips the rather trite   ↑ wheelbarrow;

for larger loads they use the freight tricycle; ↑

and for an owl chick that has fallen ← out of its nest, they use the carrying sled. ↙

(travelogue continued)

We became drowsy and have no recollection of the following hours or days. The Yeti probably tried to confuse us and the next thing we heard was, "Here it is," as he put the blanket down on the ground. When we stepped out we saw a mound with a rough gate in front of us. The words "III Balon" were chalked on the wall. Zero had delivered us at the Altay station.

The Yeti did not feel at ease at all. He kept looking around shyly and muttering, "Not to be seen! Be gone. Too many people."

"Shall I make you a large igloo so you can rest?" asked Nicolas. "Then you can creep away." But the Yeti disappeared without a word. Nicolas shrugged and knocked at the door. A troll's wife appeared.

"Good day, Boney," Nicolas said. "Isn't Cork III at home?"

"Cork sick!" she said.

"This is Cork III's original family hole. He and his wife kicked out their family after their conversion," Nicolas said to us. It was a genuine troll's den inside. A river ran through it and there were barred cells for stolen children. Two balloons hung on the ceiling. A corpulent troll lay in the corner on fir branches. When we stood near him he held his stomach, groaning. We uncovered his stomach and examined him.

"General constipation from overeating," Nicolas said. "Nothing serious. He must be properly purged."

He showed us how to make an enema-syringe and told us about a folk remedy used for such purposes. When everything was prepared, the troll's wife adminis-

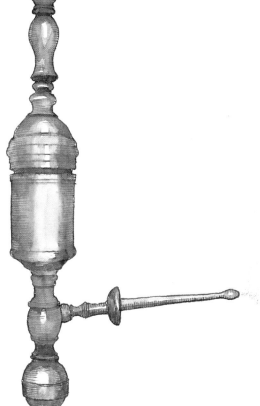

tered the apparatus. At first nothing happened. After a quarter of an hour Cork III rose from his couch and ran outside, leaving the door open. Within seconds there were noises from the forest that approached explosions. "Give him time," Nicolas said, closing the door fastidiously.

It was eight o'clock and we were hungry. Nicolas rustled up all sorts of edibles from a cupboard and made us feel we were back in the civilized world instead of in the middle of the Siberian taiga. At least we were far from the icy Arctic region and we could use a balloon again, although Nicolas had not given any indication of what was awaiting us at the Yenisey.

Cork III came back from the forest half an hour later, white around the gills and with beads of sweat on his low forehead but obviously relieved. Nicolas got him to

take a balloon outside and an hour later we were air-
borne in a moderate wind on the way to Crown Cork on
the Yenisey River near Pit-Gorodok, in the Yeniseyskiy
range.

The journey to Crown Cork went well. It took three
days and was uneventful. We once drifted over a bare
hill where an extraordinarily small moose had scraped
the snow aside and stood eating moss. He and Nicolas
exchanged greetings.

"That is One Eye, the dwarf," Nicolas said. "He has
been called that since he was a calf. I found him half-
dead in a river when he was four months old. The mosquitos had overwhelmed him, which happens here

sometimes. His eyes, nose, mouth, and ears were filled
with mosquitos, and they had bitten everything into a
bleeding mass. He had waded into the water to get rid of
them, though it didn't help much. I cleaned him up as
much as possible but his left eye couldn't be saved, so I
had to remove it. He didn't seem to be growing at all. I
managed to ferret out his mother, who had abandoned
him, and she had just enough milk in her udder to suckle
him."

Balloon Station IV was larger than the previous
three; we met some tall, broad-shouldered gnomes waiting for a favorable wind.

We put on our skis again, ready to cross the snow-
covered landscape. Crown Cork was a very old troll

The wolverene (Gulo gulo), *also called glutton or rock cat, is a mountain marten in the extreme north measuring up to three feet long. Its pelt is highly prized by the Siberians because breath does not condense inside it.*

without a tail. He wore a pair of owllike spectacles that probably had plain glass in them. Still, Nicolas said, he could read a few words and he had concocted a timetable that was pretty useless since everything depended on the wind. He behaved as if he were indispensable even for the minutest trifles and even fussed around with our skis till Nicolas commanded him to stop.

After this we left for Nicolas's house twenty-five miles away. The snowy taiga was most impressive and we crossed all kinds of animal tracks; we even saw a sable marten and a wolverene.

Circling a village in rather a wide sweep, we came across a roebuck in a trap. He was still alive but was crazed from fear and pain. Nicolas tried to calm him

down so that we could climb onto his neck and saw through the steel snare, but he kept struggling and pulling away, thereby tightening the cord.

It was a terrible sight. Blood and froth came out of the roebuck's mouth and he was thrashing about so wildly he seemed on the verge of madness. When he had calmed down a bit from sheer exhaustion we quickly climbed near the snare and took turns sawing. Two of us held the snare away from the skin while the third sawed. It was not easy to get through the plaited steel wires and the still-struggling buck was a frightful hindrance. When we reached the next-to-the-last wire, Nicolas sent us down because the buck was sure to bolt away.

The snare had barely snapped off when he made a desperate dash for freedom. With a thud Nicolas was thrown against a tree and lay there motionless. As we knelt next to him, he said without batting an eyelid, "That's a broken leg! Help take the boot off."

His shin was indeed broken. It was one of the rare cases of an animal injuring a gnome, though done inadvertently. We were surrounded by cedars, firs, spruce, birch, and mountain ash, but no elder for a splint, so we had to make do with a pair of smooth mountain-ash branches. We couldn't find arnica in the snow either, to speed up the healing. One of us pulled at the broken leg until the soles were level, while the other put the mountain-ash branches around the limb and tied them securely. It must have been agony; Nicolas did not utter a word but indulged in a few stiff swigs of brandy. We then cut off his sock and boot and bound them around his foot to keep it warm.

We were still ten miles from his home. We cut branches from a willow farther on from which we could make a stretcher and braces for ourselves. Our knapsack belts were strong enough to support the whole thing.

Nicolas growled approvingly when all was ready. We put our skis on and tried to start off gingerly. It was difficult at first and we fell a couple of times, causing scathing words from the stretcher, but gradually we managed to cover some distance. Nicolas pointed the way. Two hours later we stood under an enormous cedar that hid the entrance to his house. Just as we were about to carry him in he said, "Wait. We will never get through the revolving door like this. Get my wife."

The Siberian roe is much bigger than the European, although it has a six-tined antler.

We entered the cave, walked through a long passage, and knocked. The buxom Siberian woman who answered raced with us outside. Nicolas was standing up. She hugged him and said, "My little bear, what has happened to you?" Her name was Sofia Wladimirowna. Nicolas insisted on hobbling in. He was put to bed and we took the splints off his leg, rubbed the skin with arnica ointment, and made better splints from elder branches.

During the meal that followed he said: "I shall now put an end to your uncertainty. My compatriots were angry enough with you because of the Siberian passages in your first book to summon you to court. The journey to Lapland was enough to satisfy the western gnomes, but thereafter we wanted you in Siberia. At first Mirko was against it but he gave in when the king insisted. I had to meet you in Lapland and bring you here to study your behavior in my capacity as justice of the peace. At first uncertainty made me rude, for which I offer my apologies. The king also forbade us to let you see the whole Secret Book. You have not grumbled although you must have been consumed with curiosity to know what was going to happen; that has not passed unnoticed. In a secret message received at Crown Cork, I was given the freedom to decide whether you should be prosecuted or not; the help you gave me with my leg was the decisive factor. I have recommended that the court case be canceled. You may return home, but on three conditions. Those I shall tell you when your exhausted bodies have had eight hours sleep."

Somewhat confused, we stumbled into bed. Sofia, who seemed to think we had more or less saved her husband's life, tucked us in herself, although we were so tired we hardly noticed it.

We woke, still not completely rested, and were very soon sitting down for breakfast when Nicolas said, "And now the three conditions! One: you must take back all the dreadful things you said about Siberians in your next book. Two: you will have to complete a couple of competence tests. Three: you will take home a commission. You will be taken to a special address. I shall say nothing more than that."

We felt both melancholy and excited. What was going to happen now? Nicolas silently shook hands. When we asked if this was goodbye, he said nothing.

Sofia led us to a cave high in the mountain and left us there. We walked through a passage and reached a door decorated with a closed eye. When we knocked, the eye opened.

The door opened by itself and a big gnome with a broad smile stood in front of us. Peace radiated from his face. He said in a friendly voice: "Quite. The Dutch guests. Nicolas sent a message to expect you. Welcome to Morpheus's arms. I am the Sandman."

The Sandman in the middle of Siberia? To say we were surprised would be an understatement!

The Sandman's face was like an autumny golden apple with thousands of little wrinkles. When we were seated in easy chairs in the living room we asked him how he managed his sleep deliveries. He would not tell

us but apparently it had something to do with magic stratospheric motions that included the fourth dimension. "Just as time stands still on the edge of a black hole in the universe, so I let people drop off into timelessness," he said simply.

Later on we were allowed to take a look in his cellars, where innumerable sacks of sleep sand were piled. On some were written: "Requisites for HIBERNATION."

"Don't you have to leave to put people to sleep?" we asked.

"No," he said. "Some nights everyone has to fend for himself. I can't always be out. I'm too old. I'm as old as the world."

He told us a couple of wonderful but terribly tiring stories about famous people who had trouble falling asleep, until we became so sleepy we nearly fell off our chairs. Then with sand in our eyes we went to a wonderful bed some hours too early, embraced by the arms of Morpheus.

THE FIRST MISSION

We awoke in a tropical valley between green mountains. It was sunset and stifling hot. Where and in which time were we?

There was not a soul around to ask. We deliberated with heavy hearts. We were probably expected to do something, but what? Perhaps we had been dropped in a deserted spot to see if we remembered the rules of survival. A river ran below us. Since we had to go somewhere, it seemed wise to follow it downstream (Nicolas had taught us to do that when lost), and even more so because the water was low and it was easy walking on river sand. We were accompanied by swarms of biting

mosquitos and other flying small fry. Two crows circled high above the mountains. We made ourselves a shield against the mosquitos by tucking grass blades under the rims of our pointed caps, and we kept our hands under our beards. We suddenly noticed the gnome sign for danger in the stones on the bank: DANGER! GO TO THE LEFT! So gnomes had definitely been here! The only problem was that if we went left, our path would lead straight to the mountains and we would be completely lost. In addition, the sign looked years old and since there seemed little chance of meeting a gnome in the mountains, we decided to go gingerly on.

Since time immemorial the gnomes have worked with secret branch signals in forest and field – for example,

"general danger signal"

←

"go 300 yards to the right"

"search from right to left and back" →

or
"look out for the troll's snare"

↓

a pinecone sewn into an oak branch is almost as stupid as the troll himself,

and just as ridiculous as a pheasant cock with the tail of a blackcock

↓

(not that it has anything to do with a gnome, but it just came to mind).

gnome signs

... or a woodcock with a drake's tail,

or a roe deer with mountain goat's horns, →

or a fox with boar's teeth,

a rabbit with a long tail,

a magpie with the comb and wattle of a common or garden rooster,

a wild boar with roebuck antlers

or an innocent mother duck with the tail of a pheasant!

that sort of thing

We had not gone three hundred feet before we stupidly tumbled into a pit with vertical rock walls that had been hidden under the white river sand.

At dawn we found ourselves, black-and-blue, looking out of a cage at a sort of beardless Neolithic man who wore a loincloth and a necklace of yellow eye teeth. He picked up the cage, shook us savagely, and gave a coarse laugh. Then we were put against the wall of the living-room cell. A couple of silent women were at work and a slavish little man brought us a thick meat porridge, which we had to share with a mouse. In a niche in the rock opposite we saw a gnome couple standing on a shelf. They look disheveled and miserable.

"Hey, pssst!" the man called in gnome language. "Where have you come from?"

"From the Sandman in Siberia."

He looked at us skeptically.

"Can't you get us out of the cage?" we asked.

"We are stuck to this shelf," said the woman dismally, "and must stand in this weather house. We are the last gnomes in this country. Jaw has eaten them all or chased them away." (A witch predicted at Jaw's birth that he, the chief, would remain without children until the gnomes came to his salvation.)

The man said, "All his wives are childless. He had all the gnomes in the country rounded up and at first beseeched them to help, questioned them, then tortured them, and finally conceived the primitive plan of fattening them up and eating them in the hope of getting their potency tranferred to him. You also will be stuffed and eaten."

One of the women threw a cloth over our cage to prevent us from talking to the gnomes. By morning we had figured out a solution. When the cloth was removed at porridge-time we told Jaw we could help him with his problem. It took hours to gain his confidence until at last he agreed to our suggestions, which was that he arrange for women above child-bearing age to urinate in a stone pot. If we were freed and promised that we would not try to escape, we would arrange the rest.

We carved a primitive injection syringe from a tropical hardwood, steamed the urine gently over a low fire, and injected Jaw's hard bottom with it three times a week. The needle was much too thick, but these tough rascals were used to pain. It must be said for Jaw that he willingly underwent the treatment and became convinced that our cure would work! When Jaw's youngest wife became pregnant he was ecstatic. We could do nothing wrong. Our first request was that he set free the gnome couple from the weather house—they had to learn to walk again, poor things, but they recovered satisfactorily. Then we demanded that all other gnomes be allowed to return safely, without retribution, and they soon came back from the surrounding countryside. But we had not seen the last of Jaw. Although we had taught the wizard of the tribe how to administer the injections, Jaw insisted that we assist at the birth of his first child. We accompanied him on all his forays in the meantime and we saw elephants, lions, tigers, antelopes, and camels.

The heat, the mosquitos, the endless bloody battles with neighboring tribes, and the beating to death of bisons, and even worse, the trapping of mammoths—it all became unbearable. We spent many a wakeful hour working out how to leave without breaking our word.

Suddenly we awoke quite peacefully in bed at the Sandman's home. His laughing eyes were peering at us under the canopy and he said: "That was an easy commission for modern Westerners in a primitive land, wasn't it? Stupid of you to ignore the sign. Good that you kept your word. I called you back because it lasted more than three months—although that counted only as three days here."

That night he explained the essence of sleep, which is based on the interaction between the formatio reticularis and the gray matter, and it was scientifically indisputable. Then he told us the story of Sleeping Beauty—of the slumbering castle within impenetrable thorn hedges—in such a way that even Gustave Doré could not have illustrated more vividly. Then he told Snow White and the Seven Dwarfs, Rumpelstiltskin, and many others—always in the same fascinating fashion.

"You see," he explained, "a gnome was a perfectly normal being in the misty past when most fairy tales were created. Do you know that gnomes played an important part in recording fairy tales? Fairy tales are poeticized ancient wishes and experiences. Wrong must be punished; prisoners or bewitched must be freed; ugliness turned to beauty; dragons made harmless; stupidity and cruelty overcome. The small and clever become leaders and the gigantic become helpless. Just what we gnomes have always done.

"Naturally gnomes appear in countless stories, but since they are passed on by word of mouth—hardly anyone could read or write then—the gnome has become rather mutilated or disposed of altogether. Don't forget that many tales began in the last Stone Age and in the pre–Indo-Germanic cultures. You need not think they were created for children either! They sprang up among adults whose mental development was that of the children today. The adults listened with cocked ear and dreamy eye just as our children do."

Later he said, "Naturally our subconscious or, if you like, unconscious plays an enormous part in fairy tales, usually using the imagery of a lake or impenetrable forest. These two are symbols of the unknown dangerous world where past, present, and future are entangled and anything is possible. It is the fact that it is perfectly ordinary lake or forest that makes it so plausible. Anything you believe in exists. In your heart things are living realities so that you have no difficulty in placing them outside yourself in any landscape or surrounding. In short, you see what you want to see. If you were staying longer I'd show you around our fairy-tale world because it is so riveting, but I'll have to send that part of the Secret Book to you in Holland."

Toward morning, when our eyes had become heavy with sleep, he told a story of a very poor woodchopper and his wife and seven sons. "But that is the story of Tom Thumb!" we exclaimed.

"Of course! But Tom Thumb was not a human being. Here again we come across a corruption of words. Tom Thumb was a gnome, and none other that the famous gnome Thyme. So it was really Little Tom Thyme. I did mention once to Charles Perrault—I believe it was in 1697—that a human infant could never be only six inches tall, but he insisted on making him in his story into a little human boy. He also said that he felt embarrassed about these fairy tales, and that he only wrote them for fun, and even then under the name of his son. He thought that nobody would ever read them anyway, because of the fact that he was really a scholar."

THE SECOND MISSION

We woke up in a country laid waste by a werewolf. Villages were burned to the ground, cattle killed or stolen, game poached, people terrorized. It was the fifteenth century. The desperate population was paralyzed with fear and superstition, aggravated by the fact that the werewolf attacked at night in various places simultaneously. We were dropped in the wilderness at the edge of the country from which the beast undertook his forays and where for years no one had dared set foot. We searched for footprints but found only those of humans.

We were lucky the second night: from our tree hideout we saw the creature walking over a clearing. There was not one but three of them, and they were men with bewitched wolfskins! Since they thought no one was watching, the rogues walked upright and talked softly to one another. After this it was child's play for us: we made

a trap with homemade barbed wire stretched over it. When they came from the wilderness the next day, we attracted their attention while they were walking upright and got them to run after us once they realized that we had discovered their secret. We lured them on, walked over the trap without setting it off (we weighed so little), and waited on the other side. With ghastly curses they fell into the depths, their wolfskins remaining caught on the barbed wire.

The next day the trio was rendered harmless by two strong men and the skins were burned.

When we again awoke at the Sandman's, he came and sat on the edge of our bed and said: "Better, each time better! Almost real gnomes."

He was holding a section of the Secret Book that we had not seen. "Look," he said as he pointed to two papers sticking out of the book. "Read it!" He opened up the passages and we followed his wrinkled finger with burning curiosity: "In the warm age before the last ice age about a hundred and thirty thousand years before the last era, the gnomes tamed the savage Jaw, to the salvation of the gnomes in Asia."

Everything was minutely recorded even including our names. Farther on was the story of the werewolf in the Middle Ages. We were speechless, and the Sandman laughed at our reaction. "So you see," he said, "this should make the difficult journey to Siberia worthwhile. You had to come all the way here because I'm the only one who could put you into such a deep sleep that you could wander freely around in the past and have the opportunity to earn your honorable mention in the Secret Book!"

THE THIRD MISSION

After breakfast the Sandman pensively filled a pipe. He poured three glasses of wine. "You are about to leave," he said, giving us a wide smile. "You stood up well to the two tests to which we subjected you, but they were merely exercises. The third and most difficult test lies ahead." His face suddenly lost all its laughter lines and he said softly, "There once was a spirit in a bottle—a puny, naked, powerless spirit. He was well stored in his bottle for ages, but people let him out and now he has become a Dragon with Seven Heads. If you don't succeed in making this world-threatening monster harmless, annihilation will result."

We still did not understand what he was driving at.

"The time for the General Alarm has arrived," said the Sandman. "We tread ever narrower paths beside ever deeper precipices. The monster I mean is the DRAGON OF POLLUTION.

"Its first head is called LET THE FUTURE TAKE CARE OF ITSELF; the second, IT WILL LAST MY LIFETIME; the third, IGNORANCE IS BLISS; the fourth, AFTER US, THE DELUGE; the fifth, LET'S WAIT TILL IT HAPPENS; the sixth, IT WON'T BE ALL THAT BAD; and the seventh, COULDN'T CARE LESS."

He began to pace the room, overcome by emotion. We kept quiet. He was right. The end of the world seemed to be advancing with giant strides.

"Every gift has a plug attached," he resumed, "every utensil devours energy; nearly every river in the world has been poisoned; the oceans are filled with radioactive refuse packed in containers that will rust within a few years; the freon in aerosol sprays contaminates the stratosphere; drivers are fined for throwing garbage out of the window but not for the dangerous gases that escape from their exhaust pipes! A factory is allowed to turn a romantic brook into a black, muddy stream! I begin to wonder who is mad?"

He became more and more distressed. We could hardly recognize him. "What I observe around me is pollution of the water, depletion of the ground, suffocation of the air. Hundreds of square miles of forests disappear daily in three of the five continents; it is not only disastrous for the oxygen supply of the whole world but also for the preservation of numerous animal species that will one day only exist in zoos as poor shadows of their former selves."

He calmed down somewhat, sat down, and looking squarely at us, said, "This is your greatest battle and at the same time the commission to which you will have to dedicate the rest of your lives: call a halt to this dragon, drive him back, destroy him, or your children's children will have no future.

"This is what your situation is at present: as Nicolas already told you, we intended to take you to court and to punish you by, for example, not making you big again. I have recommended dropping that plan and giving you this mission instead. We gained confidence in you after Nicolas's report on the journey, and that simplified matters for us.

"Just as it was Mirko's job to get you to Lapland and Nicolas's to take you to the Yenisey, so it is mine, as oldest gnome in the world, to share this burden with you: reduce the number and the needs of spoiled humanity. Practice the methods you have learned from the gnomes. THIS is the essential call of the gnomes!

"Go now," he said at the end of the night. "Sleep once more in my house the sleep of the just, but then go into the world and destroy the Dragon with Seven Heads. Let no obstacle stand in your way. The present direction humanity is taking will lead into an abyss. Return! Reform!"

He went through the door carrying a candlestick and said: "Slitzweitz. May you prosper!"

THE RETURN

It was morning when we awoke, damp and shivering, having slept restlessly for twenty-four hours in a sort of slumber full of nightmares about monsters and calamities. In a wooden room, we lay naked on the floor on top of our old clothes and covered over by the duffel coats in which we had come. A stove glowed in a corner, and we got a glimpse of an unknown taiga outside. As we put our clothes on we noticed that the floor seemed a long way below us and we felt the empty place on our heads. We were normal adults again. A note lay on the table: "Follow the rising sun until one o'clock. Then you will see a village on the other side of the Yenisey. The ice is safe. Use your gnome's wisdom to avoid cracks! Once on the other side look for the fifth house from the left. Farewell! Nicolas."

Our luggage stood in the corner. Nothing was missing. We found two piles of rubles and our book, also enlarged as well as our—same size—Arctic clothes and our old pointed caps, neatly folded flat.

Our hearts were heavy and we felt disoriented. This was the irrevocable end to the most intimate contact humans had ever had with gnomes. Yet there was nothing we could do about it. We had to start, so we went out and closed the door behind us.

We were not even three hundred feet from the hut before we heard some forest workers. Since we became gnome-still, they did not see us and went noisily into a wooden shed. We walked on. The forest was one plantation, but the trunks were not close together. Our only guide was the sun, which had started as a fiery ball and then gradually faded but remained visible through the treetops.

The first rays of light filtered weakly through the trees, and we set our course by the sun as instructed by Nicolas from his sickbed. Without meaning to we found ourselves proceeding cautiously at first because we were not accustomed to being so far above the ground and could not judge every bush or snow bubble as accurately. We were also inclined to bend far forward to prevent our pointed caps from being knocked off by branches and twigs.

Nicolas, who had arranged absolutely everything, including winding our watches, must have known it would be a cloudless day.

We saw signs of wild ponies. We followed their trail, which went in our general direction until it veered to the left, preventing us from asking them for a ride.

We then followed the spoor of a moose. We got near him by moving soundlessly, but when he realized we were there he crashed off.

We understood sadly: the intimate contact we had shared with nature for so many weeks, whereby we could naturally communicate with all animals, was gone forever.

A little farther on was a clearing in the forest. Four roe deer stood near trees on the far side. Had we still been gnomes, we could have approached near enough to admire their slender brown-gray figures, but now they fled with high leaps. We were once again members of the two-legged race that they were quite justified in fearing.

Our luggage seriously hampered us in the deep snow (by our increased gravity; as gnomes we had become too used to not sinking into the snow). Nicolas had even taken this delay into account: the forest only went on till one o'clock! We stood at the top of a long slope. The broad, frozen Yenisey lay below us, its banks lined with bare scrub. We could make out a village on the far side. When we climbed down to the river and onto the icefield, we even saw tire tracks. We began the long crossing. So this was the Yenisey, one of the mightiest Siberian rivers, which empties into the Arctic Ocean.

In olden times this was a paradise for capercaillies, causing the banks to be "black" with them, but now they are largely poached. In spite of the rows of the horrible, baitless, razor-sharp hooks of the fish poachers, the depths under the ice must still house masses of sturgeon, Thymallis, Coregonus (salmon), trout, and pike. We climbed the bank on the other side and saw a village of mostly small houses and a few larger ones. We passed a sleigh and a few people who gave us inquisitive looks but who said nothing, and stopped at the fifth house. A man wearing a uniform cap stood some way away glaring at us suspiciously. The wooden house was surrounded by a well-cared-for winter garden, and all was enclosed by a wooden fence. As we approached, the door half opened. An elderly woman motioned to us.

When we were close enough, she pulled us inside quickly and closed the door. While we waited in the hall she anxiously peered at the man in the street through a window in the front. Finally she came back and said in broken German that everything was fine. She led us to the first and only story, where there were two freshly

made beds, a bowl of water, and some soap. We put
down our luggage, freshened ourselves up, and went
downstairs. Our hostess was more relaxed now. Her
name was Natasha Filipowna. She had a delicious
borscht for us with black bread and a glass of beer. We
were as hungry as hunters. It appeared from the conversation that the gnomes had arranged things here also: we
were at a distant spur of the Trans-Siberian railway, the
famous TransSib founded by the Czar Nicholas II, that
connects Moscow with Vladivostok and is over six
thousand miles long. We had to wait four days before
there was a connection from the village in Achinsk with
the TransSib, but that was the only inconvenience.

Our tickets home were all in order, as were our travel permits with stamps and all passports, and handwritten identity cards. The gnomes must have had friends even in this country. We had enough rubles for the days we were to spend on the train. Natasha told us that in order to avoid any possible trouble we would not be allowed to go into the street during these four days—the less attention we attracted, the better.

Thus we spent the next four days. Natasha looked after everything and we were content. Her late husband had been an interpreter for German prisoners during the war and she had picked up a few words. Her five children were married and lived far away. During these four days we finished our entire book and decided to offer it for publication to Jan Weggemans when we returned.

We had a long journey in front of us, and the Sandman's last words echoed in our ears. When we finally got home we would have to take his commission seriously. But even without the commission, our lives would never be the same after this unbelievable summons of the gnomes. Although we had gradually become used to our height and no longer bowed our heads to get through a door, we were still gnomes at heart. The fact that we had actually been gnomes could never be changed, even though we would soon be with our dear ones where we belonged.

While working on our book in the room upstairs in
Natasha's house we often caught each other staring out
at the vast taiga and the ice masses of the mighty Yenisey
in the distance, or pensively balancing our pointed caps
on the top of an index finger and letting them run along
the edge of the table; then, words were superfluous.

On a still, overcast day with a temperature just above freezing, we boarded the train, a symbol of bonds torn asunder. We had heard nothing more from the gnomes, though we could rest assured that they followed our doings closely. The endless trunks of the southern taiga began to slip past. There were long empty vistas deep into the forest, but we knew that trusted animals were housed there—and gnomes.

When we looked back through the window at the disappearing station shrouded in snow and mist, we thought we saw a red mark in the snow, from which, although we were ordinary people again, we received a forceful wireless message that amounted to Cicero's famous sigh:

QUO USQUE TANDEM?
How long still?

LIBRARY OF CONGRESS CATALOGING-IN-PUBLICATION DATA
Huygen, Wil.
The complete gnomes / by Rien Poortvliet and Wil Huygen.
p.   cm.
Combines the authors' Gnomes, originally published in 1977, and
Secrets of the gnomes, originally published in 1982.
ISBN 0–8109–3195–8
I. Poortvliet, Rien.   II. Huygen, Wil. Leven en werken van de
kabouter. English. 1994.   III. Huygen, Wil. Oproep der kabouters.
English. 1994.   IV. Title.
PT5881.18.U9A2   1994
839.3'186407—dc20   94–4254

Original Dutch edition published under the title *De kabouter*
Copyright © 1994 Unieboek b.v./Van Holkema & Warendorf,
The Netherlands
Illustrations copyright © 1976, 1981 Rien Poortvliet
Text copyright © 1976, 1981 Wil Huygen
English translation copyright © 1977, 1982 Unieboek b.v./Van Holkema
& Warendorf, The Netherlands

The Complete Gnomes is a one-volume edition of *Gnomes* and *Secrets
of the Gnomes*, originally published by Harry N. Abrams, Inc., in 1977
and 1982 respectively.

Published in 1994 by Harry N. Abrams, Incorporated, New York
A Times Mirror Company
All rights reserved. No part of the contents of this book may
be reproduced without the written permission of the publisher

Printed and bound in Germany

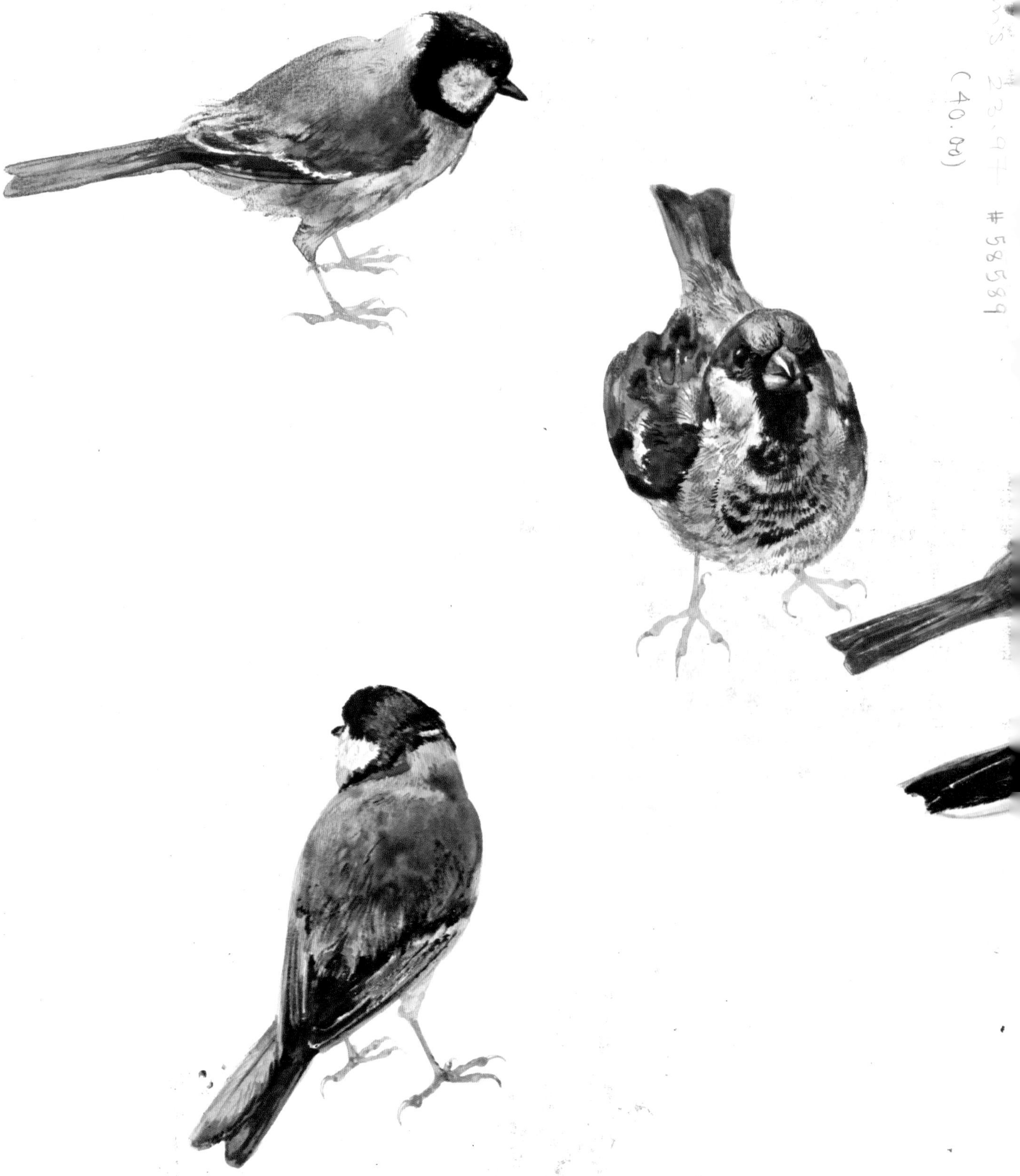

10,2694 Abrams 4 23.97 #58589 (40.00)